LAW FOR NURSES

Cavendish
Publishing
Limited

LANGDALE UNIT/
FORENSIC PSYCHIATRY
SERVICE

LAW FOR NURSES

**Gill Korgaonkar, LLM, Director of Legal Studies,
University of Hertfordshire**

**Professor Diana Tribe, LLB, MA, Head of Law,
University of Hertfordshire
Associate Research Fellow,
Institute of Advanced Legal Studies,
University of London**

Cavendish
Publishing
Limited

First published in Great Britain 1995 by Cavendish Publishing Limited, The Glass House, Wharton Street, London WC1X 9PX.

Telephone: 0171-278 8000 Facsimile: 0171-278 8080

British Library Cataloguing in Publication Data. A catalogue record for this book is available from the British Library.

Korgaonkar, G, Tribe, D
Law for Nurses

ISBN 1-85941-132-0

Printed and bound in Great Britain

Dedication

This text is dedicated to all the nurses whom we have had the pleasure of teaching at the University of Hertfordshire.

Preface

Nurses must now keep up, not only with advances in medicine and changes in the nursing role, but also with the response of the law to these changes. There have been many such changes over the past ten years which our teaching has shown are of significance to members of the nursing profession. Not all of them can be covered in a text of this size, however, we have attempted to select those areas which are likely to be of most interest and importance, and/or where there have been recent changes in the law. Many of these issues are regularly reported in the press and on television, for example the recent sad cases of child B, whose parents challenged the decision of Addenbrooke's hospital to refuse further treatment for a form of leukemia and the seriously brain damaged child whose parents are currently seeking the approval of the courts to terminate his life.

Our text commences with an introduction to the basic common law areas of liability for negligent acts and the meaning of consent. It also covers the statutory control of product liability, liability for pre-birth events, vaccine damage, human organ and tissue transplants and patients detained under the Mental Health Act. This is followed by a discussion of access to patients' records and issues of patient confidentiality. We have also included a chapter on the developing area of the law relating to the elderly which is becoming increasingly important as the number of elderly people in the population increases. The concluding chapter covers important aspects of health and safety at work legislation and incoporates the recent changes which have been brought about by the developing law of the European Union.

Each chapter is concluded by case studies which we hope our readers will find relevant to their practice experience and attempt to answer by reference to the preceding text.

The law has been stated, as far as possible, as it stood on 30th June 1995.

Contents

Table of Cases

Table of Statutes

1   Medical Negligence: General Principles

Introduction

Background

Although legal action against health professionals has a long history in English law, both the number of claims against medical practitioners, and the size of awards, have risen dramatically over the past decade. There are various reasons for this increase, however the two most popularly cited are a general increase in consumer awareness and the wider availability of legal aid (which has recently been extended to be available to children).

It is certainly the case that the numbers of lawyers specialising in medico-legal work has increased and plaintiffs now have better access to quality legal advice in this area than was the case 20 years ago. However, some patients' organisations, notably the Action for Victims of Medical Accidents, argue that there still are considerable difficulties for a plaintiff in a medical negligence case. The procedure is a costly, lengthy and cumbersome one, bedevilled by growing complexities in this area of law. However, the government's proposals for 'paper arbitration' as an alternative and simpler method of dealing with some medical negligence claims has not, to date, received widespread support.

Basic principles

Most claims against health professionals are founded in the tort of negligence (although private patients, who enjoy a contractual relationship with their doctor, may also base a claim in the law of contract). To maintain a successful action in medical negligence a plaintiff must prove:

- that the defendant (whether health professional or the employing health authority or trust) owed the plaintiff a duty of care; and,

- that the defendant was in breach of that duty; and,

- that the breach caused a type of harm which the law recognises as giving rise to damages.

Despite recent pressure for the introduction of a national 'no-fault' liability scheme, the need for a plaintiff to prove fault on the part of the defendant is an essential ingredient and is likely to remain so for the foreseeable future.

The duty of care

Definition

The classic statement defining the duty of care, which underlies all negligence claims, was made by Lord Atkin in *Donoghue v Stevenson*[1] when he said that:

> you must take reasonable care to avoid acts or omissions which you can reasonably foresee would be likely to injure your neighbour. Who, then, in law is my neighbour? The answer seems to be-persons who are so closely and directly affected by my acts that I ought reasonably to have them in contemplation as being so affected when I am directing my mind to the acts or omissions that are called in question.

This general statement of principle clearly covers the position of a doctor or nurse in relation to a patient, who by definition must be 'someone who is so closely and directly affected' by their acts that he or she ought to 'have them in contemplation'. However, specific reference to a doctor's duty of care was made in an earlier (criminal) case by Lord Hewitt when he said:

> If a person holds himself out as possessing special skill and knowledge, and he is consulted, as possessing such skill and knowledge, by or on behalf of a patient, he owes a duty to that patient ... (*R v Bateman*[2]).

To whom is the duty owed?

It is clear that a health professional who undertakes the care of a patient, whether privately or within the National Health Service owes the patient a common law duty of care. Thus a hospital doctor or a nurse owes a duty to any patient whom he treats at the hospital. Similarly, any patient who is admitted to hospital is also owed a duty of care by the health authority or trust hospital and other staff. In the same way a GP and his staff owe this duty to any patient on the GP's list and will also be liable for any treatment, voluntarily undertaken, of a patient who is not on his list but is temporarily in his locality. The same duty is also owed to patients where a doctor or nurse acts as a 'good Samaritan' (for instance in a road accident) as was explained in by Willes J in *Skelton v London North Western Railway*[3] where he said: 'if a person undertakes to perform a voluntary act he is liable if he performs it improperly.'

The Congenital Disabilities (Civil Liability) Act 1976 (which will discussed in more detail later in the text) extends the common law duty of care which is owed to a mother and/or father to include any child who is injured as a result of health professional's tort against his parents.

---

1. *Donoghue v Stevenson* [1932] AC 562.
2. *R v Bateman* [1925] 94 LJKB 791.
3. *Skelton v London North Western Railway* [1867] LR 2 CP at 636.

When does the duty arise?

It is usually relatively easy to show that a patient is owed a duty of care; the question that does sometimes arise however is when this duty comes into being. Is it as soon as the patient enters the doors of the hospital, or when he reports to the casualty receptionist, or when he first receives some form of treatment from hospital staff? In *Barnett v Chelsea and Kensington Hospital Management Committee*[4] the question arose as to whether a duty of care had been owed to three men who had entered the Casualty Department of their local hospital one New Year's Eve, complaining of vomiting. They outlined their symptoms to the nurse on duty who relayed them by telephone to the duty casualty officer who, without seeing or examining them, advised them to go home and consult their own general practitioners. One of the men subsequently died of arsenic poisoning. In discussing whether a duty of care was owed to the men, although they had not actually been seen by the doctor it was said 'This is not a case of a casualty department which closes its doors and says that no patients can be received'. The three watchman entered the defendant's hospital without hindrance, they made complaints to the nurse who received them and she in turn passed those complaints on to the medical casualty office, and he sent a message through the nurse purporting to advise the three men:

> ... In my judgment there was here such a close and direct relationship between the hospital and the watchmen that there was imposed on the hospital a duty of care which they owed to the watchmen.'

It would appear therefore that the duty of care arises at the point when patients make their presence on the premises known to the appropriate hospital staff. It is possible that hospitals without accident and emergency departments would not be under a similar obligation to patients arriving without appointment; however, in the event of a seriously ill patient presenting himself for treatment at such a hospital it is likely that there is a duty to take reasonable steps to ensure the safety of the patient, even if this only consists of summoning an ambulance, or administering first aid.

Who owes the duty of care?

Until the decision in *Cassidy v Ministry of Health*[5] the courts took the view that the duty of care to the patient, was owed by the doctor, and that the hospital was neither primarily nor vicariously liable for the acts or omissions of medical practitioners in the exercise of their professional skills. However, In *Cassidy* Lord Denning declared that this view was wrong, based as it was on a '... desire

---

4. *Barnett v Chelsea and Kensington Hospital Management Committee* [1969] 1 QB 428.
5. *Cassidy v Ministry of Health* [1951] 2 KB 343.

to relieve the charitable hospital from liabilities which they could not afford'. (No doubt the courts were also originally influenced by the problems associated with the application of the 'control test' in *Yewens v Noakes*[6] to doctors' contracts of employment, which was used to distinguish between employees and the self-employed and could not satisfactorily be applied to professional workers.) Since *Cassidy*, the courts have acted on the assumption that health authorities and trust hospitals are vicariously liable for the tortious acts of all staff employed by them (including consultant medical staff) and this assumption has gone unchallenged. Thus claims have been accepted against health authorities and hospitals (including private hospitals) in respect of alleged acts of negligence by nursing staff (*Fussell v Beddard*[7]) and radiographers (*Gold v Essex County Council*[8]); it is less clear whether there is also liability for the acts of an agency nurse, though the argument that the hospital is liable (both vicariously and primarily) seems a compelling one. The principle of vicarious liability only extends to those actions which are within the scope of the employee's contract of employment (*Iqbal v London Transport Executive*[9]), thus where it can be proved that the employee has acted outside the scope of his contract of employment (eg not during his agreed hours of employment) the hospital is not vicariously liable. However it is important to remember that an employer can be held vicariously liable even for those actions which he has expressly forbidden his employee to do (*Rose v Plenty*[10]).

A consultant or a charge nurse cannot be held vicariously liable for the negligent acts of junior doctors or nurses, since an employee cannot be liable for the actions of another employee (*Rosen v Edgar*[11]). Although the care of patients may be delegated to other staff, the duty of care itself cannot be delegated and remains the responsibility of the individual health professional. Thus in *Cole v Reading*[12] where a patient was advised to attend another hospital for treatment, but failed to do so, both the doctor and the health authority concerned were held to have been negligent in not checking that the patient had taken their advice.

The Family Health Services Authority (FHSA) is not vicariously liable for the actions of a GP, who is, in law, an independent contractor. However, the FHSA is under a duty to employ competent general practitioners and could incur liability for any failure which results in damage. GP's themselves are statutorily liable for the negligent acts of their fellow partners, as well as being vicariously liable for the acts of their nursing and other staff.

---

6. *Yewens v Noakes* [1880] 6 QBD 530.
7. *Fussell v Beddard* [1942] 2 BMJ 411.
8. *Gold v Essex County Council* [1942] 16 KIR 329.
9. *Iqbal v London Transport Executive* [1973] 1 WLR 141.
10. *Rose v Plenty* [1976] 1 WLR 141.
11. *Rosen v Edgar* [1986] 293 BMJ 552.
12. *Cole v Reading* (1963) 107 SJ 115.

Breach of the duty of care

General principles

Once a plaintiff in a medical negligence action has established that the defendant owed him a duty of care, the next step is for him to show that the defendant was in breach of that duty, ie that he was negligent. The question that arises here is 'by what standard is a doctor, or other health professional, to be judged'. In non-medical negligence cases the *dictum* of Alderson B in *Blyth v Birmingham Waterworks Co*[13] is often used as a definition:

> Negligence is the omission to do something which a reasonable man guided by those considerations which ordinarily regulate the conduct of human affairs would do or doing something which a prudent and reasonable man would not do.

However, the standard to be achieved by a health professional cannot be based on this test alone, since the 'prudent and reasonable man' obviously does not hold himself out as having any professional medical skills. Following the landmark decision in *Bolam v Friern Hospital Management Committee*[14], the standard of care which a health professional must reach is the standard of the reasonably competent practitioner in the appropriate specialism. McNair J's direction to the jury in *Bolam* was:

> ... where you get a situation which involves the use of some special skill or competence, then the test as to whether there has been negligence or not is not the test of the man on the top of the Clapham omnibus, because he has not got that special skill. The test is the standard of the ordinary skilled man exercising and professing to have that special skill. A man need not possess the highest expert skill; it is well established law that it is sufficient if he exercises the ordinary skill of an ordinary competent man exercising that particular art.

This definition has in turn been approved, summarised and paraphrased on many occasions, see eg Lord Scarman in *Sidaway v Bethlem Royal Hospital*[15] where he said:

> A (doctor) is not negligent if he acts in accordance with a practice accepted at the time as proper by a responsible body of medical opinion, even though other doctors adopt a different practice.

As a result, unlike all other claims in negligence, where the question of breach is set in relation to an objective standard, a decision as to whether a

---

13. *Blyth v Birmingham Waterworks Co* (1856) 11 Exch 781 26.
14. *Maynard v West Midlands Area Health Authority* [1985] 1 All ER 635; *Bolam v Friern Hospital Management Committee* [1957] 2 All ER 118.
15. *Sidaway v Bethlem Royal Hospital* [1985] 2 WLR 48.

health professional has been in breach of his duty of care will be made by reference to standards which are set by medical practitioners themselves and these standards may change in the light of prevailing medical knowledge.

To which areas of treatment does the test apply?

In *Sidaway*[15] the House of Lords held by a majority that the *Bolam* test was applicable to all aspects of a medical practitioner's work; thus it applies to private as well as NHS practice, and to all aspects of the professional relationship. This includes the diagnosis of symptoms, counselling, therapeutic and non-therapeutic treatment and follow-up. Obviously advances in medical knowledge between the date of the alleged negligent act and the date of the trial must be ignored in determining whether the defendant practitioner exercised reasonable skill and care at the time of the treatment. As Lord Denning said in *Roe v Minister of Health*[16]: 'We must not look at the 1947 accident with 1954 spectacles'. However, there is ample scope for a genuine difference of opinion between health professionals. One man cannot be held negligent simply because his conclusions differ from that of other medical professionals, nor because he has displayed less skill and knowledge than others more competent would have shown in the same situation.

Specialists

It has always been clear that a patient is entitled to a greater standard of care from a specialist consultant than from a house surgeon or general practitioner; this principle must also apply to nurses (eg specialist neonatal nurses). This point was clarified in *Wilsher v Essex Area Health Authority*[17] where it was held that the standard of skill and care required of medical staff related to the post which they occupied rather than to their own personal knowledge. However, as Lord Scarman pointed out in *Maynard v West Midlands Regional Health Authority*[18]: 'A doctor who professes to exercise a special skill must exercise the ordinary skill of his specialty.'

Junior staff

Lack of experience, ability or knowledge is no defence as *Jones v Manchester Corporation and Others*[19] demonstrates. The incompetent novice, whether doctor or nurse, will clearly be liable if he or she fails to obtain advice from senior staff,

---

16. *Roe v Minister of Health* [1954] 2 QB 66, CA at 487.
17. *Wilsher v Essex Area Health Authority* [1988] 1 All ER 871.
18. *Maynard v West Midlands Regional Health Authority* [1984] 1 WLR 634 at 638.
19. *Jones v Manchester Corporation and others* [1952] 2 KB 852.

and the recognition that junior hospital doctors might be negligent for failure to obtain a second opinion was clearly stated in *Payne v St Helier Group Hospital Management Committee*.[20] This standard matches that established in other areas of the law of negligence where, eg it has been held that a car driver's argument that she was doing her incompetent best was not sustainable (*Nettleship v Weston*[21]).

Patient characteristics

Where a patient has particular characteristics (eg obesity or alcoholism) which make the medical procedure more difficult or hazardous, these will be taken into account by the courts in determining liability. In *Williams v North Liverpool Hospital Management Committee*[22] a plaintiff sued as a result of suffering an abscess caused by the wrongful injection of pentothal into the arm tissue instead of the vein. The defence (which was successful) was that the plaintiff's arm was 'exceedingly fat' which made the veins much more difficult to find. The court found that the doctor could not have taken any further steps than he had to ensure the exact location.

New forms of treatment

Where normal medical procedures (eg carrying out blood tests, x-rays, etc) are not followed the courts are more likely to hold that he has been negligent if there is any resulting mishap. Similarly, where a medical practitioner departs from generally approved medical practice for no apparently good cause, and damage results, he too is likely to be held negligent. In *Clark v MacLennan and another*[23] a doctor carried out a surgical procedure on the plaintiff within a few weeks of childbirth; however, the general practice amongst gynaecologists was that this procedure would not ordinarily be performed on women until at least three months after childbirth. This departure from accepted practice was held to have been unjustifiable, and the plaintiff was therefore held liable for the resulting injury to the patient. Thus the courts set limits to the exercise of medical discretion in departing from agreed practice and in *Hunter v Hanley*[24] Lord Clyde said:

> ... in regard to allegations of deviation from ordinary professional practice ... such a devia-

---

20. *Payne v St Helier Group Hospital Management Committee* (1952) *The Times* 12 November.
21. *Nettleship v Weston* [1971] 2 QB 691.
22. *Williams v North Liverpool Hospital Management Committee* (1959) *The Times* 17 January.
23. *In Clark v MacLennan and another* [1983] 1 All ER 416.
24. *Hunter v Hanley* [1955] SC 200.

tion is not necessarily evidence of negligence ... Even a substantial deviation from normal practice may be warranted by the particular circumstances.

He went on to say that, in this situation, the plaintiff must prove that 'the course the doctor adopted is one which no professional man of ordinary skill would have taken if he had been acting with ordinary care'.

Similarly, in *Landau v Werner*[25] where a psychiatrist, as part of his psychotherapeutic treatment for the plaintiff's anxiety state, extended his consultations into the social setting by taking her out to dinners, Sellars LJ said:

A doctor might not be negligent if he tried a new technique but if he did he must justify it before the Court. If his novel or exceptional treatment had failed disastrously he could not complain if it was held that he went beyond the bounds of due care and skill as recognised generally.

In deciding whether a doctor has been in breach of his duty of care as a result of using a new or different method of treatment, the courts will take into account a variety of factors: these will include, the seriousness of the patient's condition, the effect on him of any orthodox treatment which had been tried previously and his understanding of, and attitude towards, the new treatment.

The law does recognise however, that, without the adoption of new techniques and new forms of treatment, the frontiers of medicine could never be advanced; indeed it is clearly in the public interest that this should occur. As Lord Diplock said in *Bolam*:

Those members of the public who seek medical or surgical aid would be badly served by the adoption of any legal principle that would confine the doctor to some long-established, well-tried method of treatment only.

Differing medical opinions and current medical knowledge

Where there is a difference of view as to the acceptable standard of medical care, a doctor will be deemed to have behaved reasonably if a group of his medical peers accept that what he did was 'reasonable' at the time that he acted. Even if others of his peers can be found to give evidence that in their opinion his actions were not in fact reasonable, this will not assist the plaintiff. As result medical negligence claims can provide a battleground for the evidence of competing medical experts. A question that arises here is, what is the position of the court where two sets of equally eminent expert witnesses give opposing evidence on behalf of the plaintiff and the defendant? In *Maynard v West Midlands Area Health Authority*[26]) Lord Scarman said:

... a judge's preference for one body of distinguished medical opinion to another also profes-

---

25. *Landau v Werner* [1961] 105 SJ 1008.
26. *Maynard v West Midlands Area Health Authority* [1985] 1 All ER 635.

sionally distinguished is not sufficient to establish negligence in a practitioner whose actions have received the seal of approval of those whose opinions, truthfully expressed, honestly held, were not preferred.

While a health professional has a duty to keep himself informed of major new developments in his field of specialty the courts do not impose on a doctor the requirement of 'absolute knowledge'. Therefore, the fact that one expert might have known of the latest research evidence available on a given treatment, does not mean that the failure of the defendant doctor to have acquired that knowledge will necessarily amount to negligence. Thus, in *Crawford v Board of Governors of Charing Cross Hospital*[27] the failure of an anaesthetist to be aware of research evidence published 6 months earlier which might have prevented a patient from developing brachial palsy, was held not to constitute negligence. Lord Denning, whose anxiety to place constraints on the apparent escalation of medical negligence claims is well documented (see eg his judgment in *Whitehouse v Jordan*[28]) said:

> ... it would, I think, be putting too high a burden on a medical man to say that he has to read every article appearing in the current medical press; and it would be quite wrong to suggest that a medical man is negligent because he does not at once put into operation the suggestions which some contributor or another might make in a medical journal.

However, a medical practitioner cannot 'obstinately and pig-headedly carry on with the same old technique if it has been proved to be contrary to what is really substantially the whole of informed medical opinion' (*Hunter v Hanley*). There is clearly room for debate and controversy as to the point in time when a new recommendation has become so well known that it has been widely accepted as proper medical practice, and thus become the standard of a reasonably competent practitioner in accordance with the *Bolam* test.

Public policy considerations

The insistence by the courts that the plaintiff prove fault, and their anxiety to avoid a finding in favour of the plaintiff out of sympathy for her plight, is a common thread running through medical negligence claims.

Some judges (notably Lord Denning) have also been influenced by the effects of the 'medical malpractice crisis' in the US where undesirable 'defensive medical practices' are said to have resulted from the explosion in the numbers of claims and the sizes of the awards of damages. The consequent implications for the National Health Service, if this were to happen in England, have not gone unnoticed. Indeed, in *Bolam* McNair J said (quoting Lord Denning in *Roe v Minister of Health*:

---

27. *Crawford v Board of Governors of Charing Cross Hospital* (1953) *The Times* 8 December.
28. *Whitehouse v Jordan* [1980] 1 All ER 267.

... we would be doing a disservice to the community at large if we were to impose liability on hospitals and doctors for everything that happens to go wrong. Doctors would be led to think more of their own safety than of the good of their patients.

Lord Denning, in *Whitehouse v Jordan* said:

in the interests of all we must avoid such consequences (as those in the US) in England. Not only must we avoid excessive damages. We must say, and say firmly, that in a professional man, an error of judgment is not negligent.

While the House of Lords over-ruled the Court of Appeal's reasoning in this case, it seems clear that judges *are* affected by a fear of a malpractice explosion in this country.

Thus, in the Australian case of *Whittaker v Rogers*,[29] the *Bolam* test was emphatically refused by the High Court as a test for acceptability of standards in supplying information to patients about risks inherent in medical treatment (see also p 27).

In this case the plaintiff, Mrs Whittaker, was referred to the defendant for surgery to improve the appearance, and vision, of her right eye in which she had been almost totally blind since childhood.

Mrs Whittaker questioned the defendant about the risks inherent in the proposed treatment, but was not informed that there was a 1 in 14,000 risk of sympathetic opthalmia developing in the other eye (which would leave her almost totally blind). The court held that the defendant had been negligent in failing to disclose the risk to the patient, despite the fact that it was not accepted medical practice at the time to do so.

The criteria for acceptable medical practice set out by the Australian High Court in this case are very similar to the principles of the Rights of Patients in Europe adopted by the World Health Organisation in March 1994 which declares (*inter alia*):

Patients have the right to be fully informed about their health status including the medical facts about their condition; about the proposed medical procedures, together with the potential risks and benefits of each procedure; about alternatives to the proposed procedures, including the effects of non-treatment; and about the diagnosis, prognosis and progress of treatment (Clause 2.2).

Perhaps because of the fear of a malpractice explosion, the *Bolam* test is undoubtedly favourable to the medical establishment for, as we have seen, the courts allow the medical profession to set the standard of care themselves. Whether this is for the greater good of the community at large is debateable, and the *Bolam* test is certainly not without its critics.

---

29. *Whittaker v Rogers* [1993] 4 Med LR 79.

Liability for patient self-harm and harm to others

Failure to supervise a patient who is at risk of causing harm to herself or others in consequence of her mental state may give rise to liability for breach of the duty of care. Thus in *Selfe v Ilford & District Management Committee*[30], the defendants were liable for the injuries of a 17 year old patient, a known suicide risk, who was left unattended by nurses near the open window from which he jumped.

A key factor in determining liability in such cases is whether the nursing staff had identified the patient as a risk to himself or others, and whether the supervision which followed fell below the standard of care that the plaintiff (or victim) was entitled to demand. The courts have recognised, however, that supervision cannot be constant, particularly in open psychiatric wards. Thus the relatives of a patient, with known suicidal tendencies, who makes a determined effort to avoid the supervision proffered, and succeeds in committing suicide, are unlikely to be successful in a claim for damages (see *Thorne v Northern Group Hospital Management Committee*[31]).

Where there has been a failure to identify a patient as a suicide risk (or someone likely to cause injury to others) and the supervision level provided has been inappropriate, the question of liability will be determined by reference to whether the health professionals involved had departed from the standard of care laid down in *Bolam*.

In *Hyde v Tameside AHA*[32] Lord Denning expressed the view that the law should, as a matter of public policy, discourage actions arising from suicide and attempted suicides. However, the case was not decided on this point and there must be some doubt as to whether such policy arguments would find judicial favour today.

Liability for failure to treat

A failure to act by a medical practitioner can give rise to liability in the same way that a positive act performed carelessly can. Thus the doctor who fails, when requested, to attend or examine a patient in circumstances where, on application of the Bolam test, it is negligent not to do so will be liable. However, not every failure to treat will give rise to liability. A competent patient has the absolute right to refuse to consent to any treatment, life-saving or otherwise (see

---

30. *Selfe v Ilford & District Management Committee* [1970] 114 SJ 935.
31. *Thorne v Northern Group Hospital Management Committee* [1964] 108 SJ 484.
32. *Hyde v Tameside Area Health Authority* (1981) *The Times* 16 April.

Malette v Shulman et al[33] and a health professional who withholds treatment in this situation will clearly not incur liability. Furthermore in *Re J*[34] the Court of Appeal demonstrated its reluctance to interfere in a doctor's clinical judgment. Here a doctor had indicated his unwillingness to place a severely handicapped baby on prolonged life support in the event of him suffering a subsequent life threatening event. Lord Donaldson MR said that a doctor's duty was to '... treat the patient in accordance with his own best clinical judgment, notwithstanding that other practitioners might have formed a different judgment or that the court, acting on expert evidence, might disagree with him'. Perhaps even more significantly he went on to say that 'the court had no knowledge of the competing claims to the health authority's resources and was in no position to express any view as to how it should deploy them'.

Inherent in any discussion on this topic is the concurrent issue of criminal liability, and the ethical considerations surrounding the debate on euthanasia where the case law tends to centre on handicapped neonates (see for instance *Re B (a minor)*[35]). The law surrounding these issues is not without considerable difficulty and is at least to some degree unsatisfactory.

Causation

Introduction

Even when a plaintiff has successfully established that the defendant owed him a duty of care, and that he had been in breach of that duty, it is also necessary to demonstrate that the breach did, as a matter of fact, cause the injury complained of. The burden of proof lies with the plaintiff who must prove causation on the balance of probabilities. There is some evidence that, at least in theory, the courts tend to adopt an approach towards causation issues which favours the plaintiff in medical negligence cases. This is best exemplified by Nourse LJ in *Fitzgerald v Lane*[36] when he said: 'a benevolent principle smiles on these factual uncertainties and melts them all away.'

However, as the protracted whooping cough (pertussis) litigation (see eg *Loveday v Renton*[37]) has shown there are often real difficulties for a plaintiff in establishing causation. The courts have held that it is not enough to establish that there exists a chance that the pertussis vaccine could cause brain damage.

---

33. *Malette v Shulman et al* [1988] 27 DLR (4th) 18.

34. *Re J* (1992) *Independent* 11 June.

35. *Re B (a minor)* [1981] 1 WLR 1421; *R v Cox* (1992) *The Times* 22 September.

36. *Fitzgerald v Lane* [1988] 3 WLR 356.

37. *Loveday v Renton* [1990] 1 Med LR 117.

The plaintiff must also show, on the balance of probabilities, that the vaccine caused the injury. It was also said in this case, *obiter*, that even if the plaintiff had been able to prove the causal link between the vaccine and the injury, it was also necessary to show (as we have seen) that the defendant had, in acting negligently, breached his duty of care. Such plaintiffs, it is suggested, face near insuperable difficulties.

The traditional approach to proof of causation is sometimes described as the 'but-for' test. Here the question asked is, 'But for the defendant's action, would the plaintiff have sustained the injury?' If the answer is 'no' then the defendant is said to have caused the damage. If the answer is 'yes' then the damage would have occurred in any event, and thus the defendant cannot be held liable. So, eg in *Barnett v Chelsea and Kensington Hospital Management Committee* although the court found that the defendant had acted negligently, he was still not liable for the plaintiff's death, because it was proved that the plaintiff would have died whatever course of action the defendant had pursued (there was no chance of a cyanide antidote being administered in time).

This 'but-for' test operates as a preliminary filter to exclude events which did not affect the outcome; it cannot however resolve all problems of factual causation.

Multiple causes

Difficulties arise where the damage complained of by the patient was possibly caused by a number of different factors combining together. The problem here is to determine which, if any, of these factors are legally relevant, so that the person(s) responsible for one or all of them should be liable to the plaintiff. Unfortunately, there is no simple test or formula for legal relevance.

An approach which the courts have often applied in such cases is to ask the question: 'Did the defendant's action materially contribute to the damage complained of?' Here there is no need for the plaintiff to prove that the defendant's action was the sole cause of the injury, simply that it substantially contributed towards it. Support for such a test was given in *McGhee v National Coal Board*[38] and in *Hotson v East Berkshire AHA*[39] where the question arose as to whether the defendant's failure to diagnose and treat the plaintiff's fractured femur materially contributed to the development of avascular necrosis. The House of Lords found, as a matter of fact, that the plaintiff's original injury (caused by a fall) was, on the balance of probabilities, the sole cause of the condition, thus relieving the defendant of liability. However, it was made clear that,

---

38. *McGhee v National Coal Board* [1988] AC 1074.
39. *Hotson v East Berkshire AHA* [1987] AC 750.

had the failure to diagnose and treat been a material contribution to the plaintiff's condition, even though not the sole cause, then damages *in full* would have been recoverable.

Similarly in *Wilsher v Essex AHA* the infant plaintiff, who had been born prematurely, developed retrolental fibroplasia which severely affected his eyesight. There were five possible causes of this condition, one of which was that the baby had received excess oxygen as a result of the proved negligent treatment by a junior doctor who had inserted the catheter monitoring blood oxygen levels, into a vein instead of an artery. The House of Lords held that the plaintiff had not proved that the negligent behaviour of the doctor had materially contributed to his injury; the mere fact that excess oxygen was one of a number of different factors which could have caused the blindness was not sufficient proof of causation. (A retrial was ordered to establish causation, but in fact was never heard, as an out of court settlement was subsequently reached between the parties.)

In *Kay v Ayrshire and Arran Health Board*[40] a child with meningitis was negligently given a substantial overdose of penicillin; on his recovery he was found to have become deaf. In a subsequent action for damages the plaintiff contended that, although there was no recorded case of deafness resulting from an overdose of penicillin, and although deafness is a common consequence of meningitis, nonetheless the overdose had created an increased risk of neurological damage, and thus materially contributed to the deafness. The House of Lords held that where there were two competing possible causes of damage, it could not be presumed that the defendant's act materially contributed, in the absence of proof that it was actually capable of causing such damage. Since there was no expert evidence of cases where a penicillin overdose had caused deafness, the court held that the overdose could not be held to be a contributing factor to this condition.

Where simultaneously occurring events are at issue the courts are presented with particular difficulties. In a US case, *Sindell v Abbott Laboratories*[41] it was alleged that the plaintiff had suffered a malignant growth because her mother had been treated with a particular drug during her pregnancy; the drug in question had been manufactured by a large number of pharmaceutical companies, and there was no evidence as to the identity of the manufacturer of the specific drug administered. The Supreme Court took the view that each potential defendant manufacturer should be liable in proportion to their market share of the drug at the relevant time.

---

40. *Kay v Ayrshire and Arran Health Board* [1987] 2 All ER 888.
41. *Sindell v Abbott Laboratories* [1980] 1 ALR 106.

Res ipsa loquitur

Although the burden of proving negligence rests with the plaintiff, there are circumstances when the courts are prepared to infer from the facts that the defendant has been negligent. Erle, CJ said in the leading case of *Scott v London and St Katherine Docks Co*[42]:

> There must be reasonable evidence of negligence. But where a thing is shown to be under the management of the defendant or his servants, and the accident is such as in the ordinary course of things does not happen if those who have the management use proper care, it affords reasonable evidence, in the absence of explanation by the defendants, that the accident arose from want of care.

This inference of negligence is nonetheless rebuttable and it is important to note that the maxim is neither a doctrine of law, nor does it reverse the burden of proof in the formal sense (see *Ng v Lee*[43]), but it is rather a 'rule of evidence, based on common sense, and its purpose is to enable justice to be done when the facts bearing on causation and on the care exercised by the defendants are at the outset unknown to the plaintiff and are or ought to be within the knowledge of the defendant' (*per* Lord Normand in *Barkway v South Wales Transport Company Ltd*[44]). The essential ingredients for its application are that:

- there is no evidence available to demonstrate how the accident occurred;

- the accident is of a kind which could not have occurred in the absence of negligence;

- the defendant (or his servant) was in control of the 'thing' causing the damage.

It would seem therefore, that the rule might have an important part to play in medical negligence claims (particularly where a surgical operation is alleged to have been negligently performed).

Thus in *Cassidy v Ministry of Health* Lord Denning had seemingly paved the way for the principle to be used in such cases when he said:

> If the patient had to prove that some particular doctor or nurse was negligent, he would not be able to do it, but he was not put to that impossible task. He says: 'I went into hospital to be cured of two stiff fingers. I have come out with four stiff fingers and my hand is useless. That should not have happened if due care had been used. Explain it if you can.' I am quite clearly of the opinion that that raises a *prima facie* case against the hospital authorities.

---

42. *Scott v London and St Katherine Docks Co* (1865) 3 H & C 601.
43. *Ng v Lee* [1988] RTR 298.
44. *Barkway v South Wales Transport Company Ltd* [1950] AC 185.

However, except in perhaps the most blatant of cases (eg where the surgeon amputates the healthy as opposed to the gangrenous leg) the courts have been hesitant to allow the plea of *res ipsa loquitur* to succeed. This was demonstrated by Scott LJ in *Mahon v Osborne*[45] where a patient died from an abscess caused by a packing swab which had been left inside the patient's abdomen after surgery:

> It is difficult to see how the principle of *res ipsa loquitur* can apply generally to actions for negligence against a surgeon for leaving a swab in a patient, even if in certain circumstances the presumption may arise ... To treat the maxim as applying in every case where a swab is left in the patient seems to me an error of law.

Similarly, in *Whitehouse v Jordan* Lord Denning, referring to the trial judge's conclusion that a doctor had, in his unsuccessful trial by forceps, caused the plaintiff to suffer cerebral palsy and was therefore negligent, said:

> The first sentence (of the judgment) suggests that, because the baby suffered damage, therefore Mr Jordan was at fault. In other words res ipsa loquitur. That would be an error. In a high-risk case, damage during birth is quite possible even though all care is used. No inference of negligence can be drawn from it.

Similarly, in *Ludlow v Swindon HA*[46] where a plaintiff claimed that she had suffered intense pain during a caesarian section operation through negligent administration of the anaesthetic, she failed to establish an inference of negligence and her claim, based on the *res ipsa loquitur* principle, was unsuccessful.

Despite these decisions, the plea of *res ipsa loquitur* has been successful in some more recent medical negligence cases. Thus in *Saunders v Leeds Western HA and Another*[47] a four year old child who suffered a cardiac arrest while undergoing surgery did not need to show the specific cause of the cardiac arrest. She was entitled to infer that the monitoring was inadequate and, in the absence of the defendants' offering an acceptable explanation, was successful in her claim for damages. So too, in *Leckie v Brent and Harrow AHA*[48] the court held that the 1.5 cm cut sustained to the plaintiff's cheek while her mother was undergoing a caesarian section could not have occurred but for the surgeon's negligence.

The principle of causation is, as has been demonstrated, an important and at times difficult concept. While a plaintiff may be able to prove negligence on the part of a defendant, it often happens that he cannot prove causation and thus fails to be compensated; the adoption of a no-fault liability scheme would not signal the end to this problem, it would merely obviate the necessity to prove that there has been a breach of the duty of care.

---

45. *Mahon v Osborne* [1939] 2 KB 14.
46. *Ludlow v Swindon Health Authority* [1989] Med LR 104.
47. *Saunders v Leeds Western Health Authority and another* (1986) PMILL Vol 1 No 10.
48. *Leckie v Brent and Harrow Area Health Authority* (1982) *The Lancet* 634.

Remoteness of damage

Even if the defendant's negligent act is proved to have caused the damage complained of, liability can still be excluded on the grounds that it was too remote; that is, that the damage:

- was more extensive; or

- was of a different type; or

- occurred in a different manner from that which would normally be foreseen.

The decisions in *Re Polemis*[49] and *The Wagon Mound (No 1)*[50] imply that the damage complained of must be a direct and reasonably foreseeable consequence of the plaintiff's act. However, it is clear from the case law that the requirement of foreseeability is not dependant on proof that the precise extent of the damage was foreseeable.

As Lord Denning explained:

> It is not necessary that the precise concatenation of circumstances should be envisaged. If the consequence was one which any reasonable person might foresee (and was not of an entirely different kind which no one would anticipate) then it is within the rule that a person who has been guilty of negligence is liable for the consequences.

An exception to the foreseeability rule, however, is the well-established principle that the defendant must 'take his victim as he finds him' (the thin skull rule). Thus in *Robinson v Post Office*[51] the defendant doctor, contrary to established medical practice, administered an injection of anti-tetanus serum to a patient, without first giving him a test dose. The patient, who was allergic to the serum, sustained severe brain damage, and the doctor would certainly have been held liable for his patient's injuries, even though they had not been foreseeable, had there not been a break in the chain of causation.

Contributory negligence

General principles

The defence that the plaintiff's injuries, though caused partly by the fault of the defendant, were also in part caused by the plaintiff's own negligence, originally absolved the defendant of all liability if it was pleaded successfully. However

---

49. *Re Polemis* [1921] 3 KB 560.

50. *The Wagon Mound (No 1)* [1961] AC 388 PC.

51. *Robinson v Post Office* [1974] 1 WLR 1176.

the Law Reform (Contributory Negligence) Act 1945 provides that compensation may be reduced in a proportion which the court thinks just and equitable, having regard to the plaintiff's share of responsibility for the damage (s 4).

This defence, though of general applicability in the law of tort is rarely used in medical negligence cases. Indeed, there is not a single English case where the defence has been successful. A possible explanation for this may be, as Picard suggests, that 'the seemingly unequal position of the parties, in that the plaintiff patient may have been ill, submissive or incapable of acting in his own best interests; (this) has led the courts to set the standard of care that patients must meet for their own care at an unreasonably low level'. However, the author goes on to say:

> As patients strive for a more equal role in their medical care and for taking aggressive steps in their own treatment, it is predictable and just that there will be more patients found to be contributorily negligent with a consequential reduction in the compensation that they will receive.

The defence of contributory negligence might conceivably be raised in a situation where a patient has failed to disclose a relevant fact to his doctor, fails to return for further treatment, or fails to co-operate in a prescribed drug regime. It is arguable, however, that patient non-compliance is reasonably foreseeable, and therefore, if there is negligence on the doctor's part his liability ought not to be reduced by the plaintiff's own behaviour. Thus in *Cole v Reading*[52] where a patient was advised to attend another hospital for treatment but failed to do so, both the doctor and the health authority were held to have been negligent in not checking that the patient had taken their advice. There was no suggestion in this case that the plaintiff had been contributorily negligent. Moreover, in *Patel v Adyha*[53], a GP who had negligently failed to diagnose a tubercular spine was unsuccessful in his argument that the plaintiff had been contributorily negligent in not seeking further medical advice.

A good example of a medical negligence case where the defence succeeded is provided by the Canadian case of *Crossman v Stewart*[54] where the plaintiff suffered irreversible eye damage caused by the prolonged use of the anti malarial drug chloroquine. The defendant had originally prescribed the drug for the plaintiff but she continued to use it for a period of two years without medical advice, after receiving a supply from a salesman. The plaintiff was held to have been two-thirds to blame for her injuries.

Similarly, in the US case of *Schleisman v Fisher*[55] the Californian Court of Appeal held that the failure of the trial judge to instruct the jury on the issue of

---

52. *Cole v Reading* (1963) 107 SJ 115.
53. *Patel v Adyha* (1985) 2 April, CA (unreported).
54. *Crossman v Stewart* (1977) 5 CCLT 45.
55. *Schleisman v Fisher* (1979) 158 Cal Rptr 527.

the plaintiff's contributory negligence (the plaintiff was diabetic and developed gangrene after failing to follow the diet prescribed by the doctor) denied the defendant's an essential defence.

Damages for nervous shock caused by medical negligence

Where the negligence of a defendant causes injury to a (primary) plaintiff which in turn causes a (secondary) plaintiff to suffer from psychiatric illness, that secondary plaintiff will not automatically be entitled to recover damages from the defendant to compensate him for the psychiatric illness he has suffered. Indeed it is now generally accepted, following the decision of the House of Lords in the case that followed the Hillsborough disaster (*Alcock & others v Chief Constable of S Yorks*[56]) that even though the risk of psychiatric illness would have been reasonably foreseeable by the defendant the law will be slow to award damages to such a plaintiff.

Thus where a doctor negligently causes the death of his patient although there will be many people who will be affected by feelings of profound sadness as a result of such negligence, it will only be in the most limited of circumstances that such plaintiffs will receive compensation through the courts.

The limited circumstances in which compensation to a secondary victim (such as a patient's spouse or parent) will normally be awarded, is where that plaintiff can prove that as a result of the defendant's negligence he is suffering from a recognised psychiatric illness which was caused by a sudden shock to the nervous system; 'shock' here is interpreted to mean the sudden appreciation by sight or sound or a horrifying event which violently agitates the mind. 'It does not include psychiatric illness caused by the accumulation over a period of time of more gradual assaults on the nervous system' (*per* Lord Ackner).

In addition the law requires that there should be 'a reasonable degree of proximity' between the plaintiff and the deceased (ie parent, child, wife).

Two recent cases are of particular relevance to the medical profession. In one, *Sion v Hampstead HA*[57] the plaintiff claimed damages from a health authority for the nervous shock he suffered as a result of observing his son deteriorate and die over a period of 14 days. As a result of this experience he suffered a very prolonged and persistent grief reaction, characterised by profound depression, disturbed sleep, impaired appetite and loss of weight, almost constant intrusive memories of all aspects of his son's life and in particular, the circumstances of his death and his own experiences at the bedside of the deceased.

---

56. *Alcock & others v Chief Constable of S Yorks* [1992] 1 AC 310.
57. *Sion v Hampstead HA* (1994) 5 Led LR 170.

The defendant health authority argued that the father's distress, suffered over a period of 14 days, could not in law amount to true 'nervous shock' since it lacked the sudden and shocking characteristics required by the law. The Court of Appeal agreed and held that the plaintiff had been made ill by a process continuing over a period of time from the father's first arrival at the hospital after his son had been injured, to his eventual appreciation of the fact that his son's death had been caused by medical negligence (which did not occur until well after the inquest). Such a process could not amount in law to 'nervous shock' and thus the father's claim for compensation failed.

However, in a more recent case, *Tredget and Tredget v Bexley HA*[58] there was also a claim for damages for psychiatric illness; this time the claim arose out of the death of a neonate where, it was claimed, both parents had suffered from nervous shock caused by the horrific circumstances of their baby's birth and subsequent death. Mrs Tredget was an insulin dependent diabetic, whose labour was obstructed by foeto-pelvic disproportion; the traumatic vaginal delivery (which involved fracture of the baby's shoulder bone) caused the 9lb 10oz baby to be delivered in a severely asphyxiated condition, with no heart beat detectable. The baby was then resuscitated and taken to the special care unit where he died two days later.

The plaintiffs claimed that the child should have been delivered much earlier in the labour by Caesarian section, and that the negligence of the hospital in permitting a vaginal delivery to take place, caused the injury and subsequent death of the baby, which in turn caused the nervous shock in respect of which the plaintiffs claimed.

Despite the decision in *Sion v Hampstead HA* referred to above, the plaintiffs claim in this case was successful. The judge (White J) held that as parents of the dead baby there was a sufficient degree of proximity between the plaintiffs and the deceased as required by the law; second he held that it was clear that the parents were suffering from a recognised psychiatric illness (a pathological grief reaction) caused as a result of an event which was frightening and horrifying and which caused shock in both parents, in the sense of their having a sudden appreciation by sight or sound which violently agitated their minds. The subsequent trial on quantum was settled with total damages of £300,000 being awarded.

The decision in the case was based upon an earlier case *Kralj v McGrath*[59] where a mother who suffered post traumatic stress disorder following the negligent delivery and subsequent death of her son was awarded £10,000 in damages.

---

58. *Tredget and Tredget v Bexley HA* [1994] 5 Med LR 178.

59. *Kralj v McGrath* [1986] 1 All ER 54.

The law has developed considerably since the conservative decisions of the courts in the early nervous shock cases at the beginning of this century. The decisions in *McLoughlin v O'Brian*[60] and *Alcock & others v Chief Constable of S Yorks*[61] have undoubtedly enlarged the range of potential plaintiffs who can claim compensation for nervous shock caused by a defendant's negligence, however the difficult legal requirement that the plaintiff must prove his illness to have been the direct result of a sudden and horrifying shock, has remained unchanged.

Clearly most deaths, whether caused by negligence or not, will be followed by the grief and unhappiness of relatives and friends. The law is clear that such unhappiness is only capable of compensation where:

- it can be classified as a recognised psychiatric illness;

- a person of reasonable fortitude would have suffered psychiatric illness as a result of a similar shock;

- the plaintiff is a close relation;

- the illness is caused by a sudden and horrifying event;

- the event was observed through the unaided senses of the plaintiff;

- the defendant's negligent act has caused the event.

Whether in the case of *Tredget and Tredget* these requirements were in truth satisfied is less than clear. Certainly the plaintiffs were proved to be suffering from a recognised psychiatric illness in respect of a the death of a close relative; certainly they observed the 'event' through their own unaided senses which was caused by the defendant's negligent act.

What is less clear however, is whether a person of reasonable fortitude would have suffered similar shock, given the circumstances, and it is even less clear that the illness was caused by a sudden and horrifying event. Rather, from the facts of the case, it would appear that the protracted events covering the induction, labour, delivery, resuscitation and death of the child over a period of 48 hours were the cause of the plaintiffs' illness.

It is suggested that, on the facts, the father in *Sion v Hampstead HA* was a more deserving plaintiff since his experience was probably even more horrifying than that suffered by the plaintiffs in *Tredget*. In *Sion* the father observed his 23 year old son deteriorate gradually from consciousness and lucidity immediately after admission to hospital, to heart attack, then to coma and finally to death over a period of 14 days; he remained uncompensated because the events

---

60. *McLoughlin v O'Brian* [1982] 2 All ER 298.
61. *Alcock v Chief Constable S Yorks Police* [1992] 1 AC 310.

21

were not sudden and horrific (as required by the law) but rather prolonged and horrific.

However, the decisions in *Kralj v McGrath* and *Tredget and Tredget v Bexley HA* make it likely that in future there will be an increasing number of such claims from parents following the neonatal death of their children caused by the negligence of health professionals. At present the maximum compensation which can be awarded under the statutory bereavement award (Fatal Accidents Act 1982) is £7,500 (raised in 1990 from the original figure of £3,500) while in the *Tredget* case the sum awarded by way compensation was £300,000 – a considerable difference. Such increased awards would obviously have a serious financial impact on health authorities who, since the introduction of Crown indemnity in 1990, are fully liable for the negligent acts of their staff, or on the insurers of doctors in private practice.

The Law Commission has recently published a consultation paper on 'Liability for Psychiatric Illness' which reviews the current law in this area and suggests that the law in certain cases is too restrictive and should be relaxed. We may thus see changes to the law governing 'nervous shock' in the not too distant future.

CASE STUDY 1

Mrs Mason was admitted to a general hospital ward for a cholecystectomy on 1 November; the admission procedures were carried out by a named registered general nurse who was to be responsible for her care while in hospital.

Mr Mason told another nurse in confidence that his wife had threatened two days before to commit suicide, but this fact was not noted in the Kardex, nor was it passed on to another member of staff.

The following evening it was noted by ward staff that Mrs Mason was withdrawn and she was reassured about her operation on the following day. Later that evening during the drugs round it was found that the patient was missing from the ward and later it was discovered that she had jumped from a fourth floor window and sustained serious injuries.

Consider the liability of the nurses involved.

CASE STUDY 2

Mr Jones was a patient on a general ward having sustained a CVA some two months previously. It was decided by his consultant, that Mr Jones would be able to begin to go home at weekends as a preparation for his eventual discharge.

On the following Friday afternoon Mrs Jones came to collect her husband from the ward; she was given three bottles of tablets with instructions as to when her husband should take them. These tablets had been dispensed from the drug trolley by the staff nurse in charge who mistakenly provided the patient with too few nifedipine tablets. Mr and Mrs Jones were driven home by the local ambulance service.

By Saturday evening Mrs Jones realised that there were no more nifedipine tablets left in the bottle. She rang the hospital and was told to return to collect some more. However, the hospital was some three miles from her home, she had no transport, and she was afraid to leave her husband alone.

The following day at about 4pm Mr Jones suffered a further CVA.

Consider the liability of the nurse and the doctor concerned.

CASE STUDY 3

On 22 March Mrs West went into hospital to have her third child. At about 11pm she was given an injection of pethidine by the midwife, on the inner side of her right thigh.

On the following day Mrs West complained of paraesthesia of the right leg distal to the injection site of the pethidine. It transpired that the injection had damaged a superficial nerve leaving Mrs West with an area of numbness in her right leg extending from the injection site to her ankle.

Consider the liability of the midwife.

2   Consent to Treatment

Every human being of adult years and sound mind has a right to determine what shall be done with his own body; and a surgeon who performs an operation without his patient's consent commits an assault ... (*per* Cardozo J in *Schloendorf v Society of New York Hospital*[1]).

What is treatment?

The expression 'treatment' is used here to cover a wide variety of health care strategies ranging from main line diagnosis and treatment of disease and injury by physical or clinical procedures, to para-medical treatments by physiotherapists, chiropractors, hydrotherapists and the like. 'Treatment' may not necessarily involve bodily contact, as is sometimes the case in the field of psychiatry, or in the administration of drugs, but whatever form the treatment takes it requires consent from the patient (or in rare cases from her representative see p 111 below).

The legal context of treatment

Where treatment is carried out unlawfully ie without the consent of the patient (or her representative), this may give rise to a legal cause of action by the plaintiff against the health professional providing the treatment. Such causes of action may either lie in the law of tort (the civil law) or amount to crimes for which the health professional may be prosecuted.

Torts

The intentional torts of assault and battery, and the tort of negligence are those which may give rise to a civil cause of action by a patient against a health professional who it is alleged has treated a patient without her consent.

Assault and battery are intentional torts which were defined by Goff LJ as follows:

An assault is an act which causes another person to apprehend the infliction of immediate unlawful force on his person; a battery is the actual infliction of unlawful force on another person (*Collins v Wilcock*[2]).

---

1.   *Schloendorf v Society of New York Hospital* (1914) 105 NE 92.
2.   *Collins v Wilcock* [1984] 3 All ER 374.

Clearly medical treatment is more likely to constitute a battery than an assault, since treatment frequently involves direct physical contact with the patient.

There are certain advantages to a patient whose cause of action is based on an intentional tort, the first one being that where a plaintiff sues in assault or battery she is not required to prove that she has suffered any specific physical injury. Thus in *Malette v Shulman*[3] a blood transfusion which saved the patient's life still amounted to a battery when performed without consent, even though it caused her no identifiable injury. Secondly, it is not necessary for the patient to prove that consent would have been refused if sought and, thirdly, the defendant is liable for all the damage which is directly caused by the act, whereas in the tort of negligence the defendant is only liable for damage that is reasonably foreseeable.

There has, however, been a clear preference by the judiciary for actions based on lack of consent to be dealt with under the tort of negligence, and in *Chatterton v Gerson*[4] Bristow J held that:

> ... it would be very much against the interests of justice if actions which are really based on a failure by the doctor to perform his duty adequately to inform, were pleaded in trespass.

Where an action is based in negligence, the plaintiff must, of course, prove that she has suffered harm as a result of the defendant's breach of duty.

The duty of care owed by a doctor or other health professional as defined in the *Bolam* test (see Chapter 1) applies just as much to the provision of proper and adequate information to patients as it does to diagnosis and treatment. If this issue was ever in doubt in was finally settled by the House of Lords decision in *Sidaway v Bethlem Royal Hospital Governors*[5] in 1985. In this case Mrs Amy Sidaway was advised to have an operation to alleviate the chronic neck and shoulder pain from which she had suffered for some time. She was warned of the possibility of disturbing a nerve root in the course of the operation, however the doctor did not warn her of the very small (less than 1 per cent) risk of damage to the spinal chord. In the event Mrs Sidaway did suffer damage to her spinal chord which left her severely disabled. She sued her doctor in negligence, *not* because the operation had been carried out carelessly, but rather because she claimed that the doctor had been negligent in failing to inform her of the small element of risk inherent in the procedure. She argued that had she been aware of the risk she would not have given her consent to the operation.

In this case the House of Lords held that the proper test to determine whether the doctor had fulfilled his duty of care to Mrs Sidaway was the *Bolam* test (see Chapter 1). In applying the test, Lord Diplock (with whom Lord Keith

---

3.   *Malette v Shulman* (1990) 67 DLR (4th) 321 (Ont CA).

4.   *Chatterton v Gerson* [1981] QB 432.

5.   *Sidaway v Bethlem Royal Hospital Governors* [1985] 1 AC 582.

and Lord Bridge agreed) said that:

> the expert witnesses specialising in neurology agreed that there was a responsible body of medical opinion which would have undertaken the operation at the time ... and would have warned the patient of the risk involved in the operation in substantially the same terms ... as the neurosurgeon had done ie without specific reference to risk of injuring the spinal chord.

Lord Bridge did add, however, that there might be circumstances where 'the disclosure of a particular risk was so obviously necessary to an informed choice on the part of the patient that no reasonably prudent medical man would fail to make it'. These 'grave adverse consequences' should always be revealed to a patient unless there were some 'cogent clinical reason why the patient should not be informed'. This situation was illustrated by Lord Templeman when he stated that because 'some information might confuse, other information might alarm, a particular patient' a doctor might not consider it to be in the patient's best interests to reveal it.

Thus, in English law the decision about the extent of information to be offered to a patient would still appear to lie in the hands of the medical profession. This situation should be contrasted with that currently prevailing in many US states where following the decision in *Canterbury v Spence*[6] a doctor must reveal to his patient all those material risks of which a reasonably prudent patient would wish to be informed. This is subject however to the defence of 'therapeutic privilege' where a doctor may decline to disclose a risk to a patient on the grounds that disclosure itself poses such a risk to the patient as to be contraindicated from a medical point of view. A similar test is applied in Canada (see *Reible v Hughes*[7]).

The position where the patient ask specific questions of his doctor about a proposed procedure is less clear. In Sidaway Lord Bridge was of the view that those questions must be answered 'both truthfully and as fully as the questioner requires' However, two years later in *Blyth v Bloomsbury Health Authority*[8] Kerr LJ appeared to disagree with Lord Bridge when he stated that:

> the question of what a plaintiff should be told in answer to a general enquiry cannot be divorced from the *Bolam* test any more than when no such enquiry is made ... indeed I am not convinced that the *Bolam* test is irrelevant even in relation to the question of what answers are properly to be given to specific enquiries, or that Lord Bridge or Lord Diplock intended to hold otherwise.

The Australian High Court considered this issue in the case of *Rogers v Whitaker*[9]) here the plaintiff who had been blind in her right eye since childhood was advised by her doctor that an operation on this eye would improve her

---

6. *Canterbury v Spence* (1972) 464 F 2d 772 (USCA, District of Columbia).
7. *Reible v Hughes* (1980) 114 DLR (3d) 1.
8. *Blyth v Bloomsbury HA* (1989) 5 PN 167; [1993] 4 Med LR 151.
9. *Rogers v Whittaker* (1992) 109 ALR 625.

vision. Naturally the plaintiff was extremely cautious about such an operation, and 'incessantly' questioned the doctor about its risks. However, the doctor failed to reveal to the plaintiff that there was a 1 in 14,000 chance of sympathetic ophthalmia developing in the 'good' left eye as a result of the operation on her right eye, and in fact despite the procedure having been carried out with reasonable skill and care, this is precisely what occurred. The doctor gave evidence that there was a responsible body of medical opinion that would not have revealed so small a risk to the patient; the patient gave evidence from other medical experts that they would have warned of the risk.

The Australian High Court specifically declined to follow the *Bolam* test as applied in *Sidaway* and found that the defendant had been negligent in failing to warn the plaintiff of the risk to her 'good' eye. The question was not whether the defendant's conduct accorded with normal medical practice, but rather whether it conformed to the standard of reasonable care which the law requires; this was a question of law to be decided by the courts rather than a question of fact to be decided by the profession. The court held, approving *F v R*[10] that the legal test for the disclosure of information was that all material risks, to which the 'reasonably prudent patient' would attach significance, should be revealed. As King CJ stated in *F v R*:

> professions may adopt unreasonable practices. Practices may develop in professions, particularly as to disclosure, not because they serve the interests of the clients, but because they protect the interests or conveniences of members of the profession. The court has an obligation to scrutinise professional practices to ensure that they accord with the standard of reasonableness imposed by the law ... This is a question for the court and the duty of deciding it cannot be delegated to any profession or group in the community.

Crimes

This chapter would not be complete without a brief reference to those crimes which may be committed by a health professional carrying out medical treatment on a patient without her consent.

The most significant offences include common assault and battery, assault occasioning actual bodily harm (Offences Against the Person Act 1861, s 47) malicious wounding or inflicting grievous bodily harm (Offences Against the Person Act 1861, s 20) and wounding with intent to cause grievous bodily harm (Offences Against the Person Act 1861, s 18). The mental element (*mens rea*) required for the commission of these offences is not considered here, although it should be mentioned that a lack of such a mental element might in fact permit a defendant to avoid criminal liability where he would, nonetheless remain liable in tort.

---

10. *F v R* (1983) 33 SASR 543.

When is treatment unlawful?

Doctors and nurses are often surprised to discover that treatment involving physical contact with patients is capable of being classified either as a tort or as a crime, if it is not carried out in circumstances which make it lawful. They reason that since their acts are manifestly intended to be in the best interests of the patient and done without 'hostile intention', no cause of action should arise. However, in the case of a competent adult patient, any medical diagnosis or treatment which involves the direct application of force which is performed without her consent, amounts to battery and/or negligence.

This issue was considered in the 1986 case of *Wilson v Pringle*[11] where the Court of Appeal held that the tort of battery must be accompanied by a 'hostile' intent which may be 'imputed from the circumstances' of the case. If this decision represented the law it would provide health professionals with a good defence since it is extremely unusual for their actions to be motivated by hostility; however more recent decisions, notably that of the House of Lords in *Re F*[12] have disapproved *Wilson v Pringle*. The effect of *Re F* therefore, is that a health professional may be found liable in tort for treating a patient without her consent, even where there is no evidence of hostile intent.

A clear statement of the requirement for consent can be found in a Court of Appeal decision in 1981: 'We think it can be taken as a starting point that it is an essential element of an assault that an act is done contrary to the will and without the consent of the victim'[13]. More recently in In *Re T*[14] Lord Donaldson MR held that 'the law requires that an adult patient who is mentally and physically capable of exercising choice must consent if medical treatment is to be lawful, although that consent need not be in writing and may sometimes be inferred from the patient's conduct in the context of the surrounding circumstances'. The legal principle underlying this approach was considered in *Malette v Shulman*[15] a Canadian case, where it was held that what was at issue was the freedom of the individual to exercise the right to consent to treatment.

> The right to determine what shall be done with one's body is a fundamental right in our society ... the bedrock on which the principles of self determination and individual autonomy are based. Free individual choice in matters affecting this right should ... be accorded very high priority (*per* Robins JA).

Similarly, it is well established that a competent adult patient has an absolute right to refuse treatment even if the effect of refusal is that the patient will die.

---

11. *Wilson v Pringle* [1986] 2 All ER 440.
12. *Re F* [1990] 2 *AC 1 (HL)*.
13. *Chatterton v Gerson* [1981] QB 432.
14. *Re T* [1992] 4 All ER 649.
15. *Malette v Shulman* (1990) 67 DLR (4th) 321.

If a patient is capable of making a decision on whether to permit treatment and decides not to permit it, his choice must be obeyed, even if on an objective view it is contrary to his interests. A doctor has no right to proceed in the face of objection, even if it is plain to all, including the patient, that adverse consequences and even death may ensue (*per* Lord Mustill in *Airedale NHS Trust v Bland*[16]).

However, in the much criticised case of *Re S (Adult: Refusal of Medical Treatment)*[17] this principle was questioned. In this case the Bloomsbury and Islington Health Authority applied for a declaration to authorise an emergency caesarian operation on Mrs S, a 30 year old woman in labour with her third pregnancy. She was admitted to hospital with ruptured membranes and in spontaneous labour; there was a grave risk of rupture of the uterus as the baby was in transverse lie with the elbow projecting through the cervix and the head lying to the right hand side.

Surgeons had done their best to persuade the mother that the only means of saving her life and that of her unborn child was to perform a caesarian operation, but she refused to consent to this treatment. Following a 48 minute summary court process of which the hearing and judgment took about 19 minutes, Sir Stephen Brown, President of the Family Division of the High Court, granted a declaration that it would be lawful to operate on the patient and provide any necessary consequential treatment, because it was in the 'vital interests of the patient and her unborn child' to do so: he based this decision on two previous cases.

The first case, *Re T (Adult: Refusal of Medical Treatment)*[18] concerned a 34 week pregnant woman who had been injured in a road traffic accident. When admitted to hospital she was discovered to be suffering from pneumonia as well as the effects of the accident, and the breathing problems that this caused resulted in the doctor's recommendation that a caesarian section be performed to deliver the baby. The child was stillborn and the mother transferred to the Intensive Care Unit where it was thought necessary that she be given a blood transfusion, which she refused.

At first instance Ward J found that the decision of Miss T to refuse live saving treatment did not extend to the emergency in which she now found herself; there was no settled intention on her part to persist in the refusal of life saving treatment; and that since by this time she was so ill she was not capable of either giving or refusing consent to life saving treatment 'it shall be lawful for the hospital, in the circumstances prevailing, to administer blood to her, that being in her best interests'.

---

16. *Airedale NHS Trust v Bland* [1993] 1 All ER 821.

17. *Re S (Adult: Refusal of Medical Treatment)* [1992] 4 All ER 671.

18. *Re T (Adult; refusal of treatment)* [1993] Fam 95.

On appeal Lord Donaldson commented that while a competent adult has the right to choose whether to accept or reject medical treatment, there is a possible qualification to this where such choice may lead to the death of a viable foetus, thus supporting the decision in *Re S*.

However, the second case (*Re AC*[19]) to which Sir Stephen Brown referred in *Re S* does not seem to support his conclusion that a competent patient could be forced to undergo surgery against her wishes where the life of a foetus is at stake; the first instance decision in *Re AC* was reversed on appeal and the patient eventually received substantial negotiated damages from the defendant.

Explicit consent

To what treatment can consent legally be given?

There has always been a general restriction on the grounds of social policy about the acts of personal violence to which a person can consent. Thus such acts as whipping for sexual gratification (*R v Donovan*)[20] and prize fighting (*R v Coney*)[21] do not fall within the lawful activities to which consent can be given.

Where medical treatment is concerned, social policy considerations have also been influential; thus it was thought at one time that it was not possible to consent legally to a sterilisation operation (see for instance Lord Denning's judgment in *Bravery v Bravery*[22] although now of course such operations can be carried out lawfully under the National Health Service (Family Planning Amendment Act) 1972. A male patient may now, it seems, consent to castration (*R v Mental Health Commission ex p W*)[23] although on the other hand female circumcision is prohibited by the Female Circumcision Act 1985.

Capacity to consent

Clearly the patient's consent to treatment must be given of her own free will and in a prison or mental institution environment this my be hard to determine (see eg *Freeman v Home Office*[24]). There have also been cases such as *Re T* where it appears that a patient's intention is overborne by a relative or other person exercising undue influence, and thus the apparent statement of intention by the patient is not, in law, freely given.

---

19. *Re AC* (1990) 573 A 2d 1253.

20. *R v Donovan* [1934] 2 KB 498.

21. *R v Coney* (1882) 8 QBD 534.

22. *Bravery v Bravery* [1954] 3 All ER 59

23. *R v Mental Health Commissioner ex p W* (1988) *The Times*, 27 May.

24. *Freeman v Home Office* [1984] 1 All ER 1036.

A doctor must also be sure that his patient has the capacity to give consent to the specific treatment offered. Incompetence is often associated with mental illness (although note that detention under the provisions of the Mental Health Act does not necessarily imply incompetence).

To be capable of giving or withholding real consent, it is usually suggested that a patient should be able to understand the nature of her illness and of the treatment proposed; however, the meaning of 'understanding' in relation to consent has been the subject of some dispute. Must the patient in fact understand that she is clinically regarded as ill and in need of treatment and in fact recognise the consequences of not having the proposed treatment, or is it merely sufficient that she is capable of understanding although she may not do so in this particular situation. It would appear that what the law requires is only that the patient is capable of understanding. The difficulties of proving actual understanding in what may be a situation of medical emergency, are obvious. There is the added point that the patient's actual understanding will in fact depend upon the quality of information provided by the doctor.

What is the effect of fraud or misrepresentation?

Clearly where a patient is misled either accidentally or deliberately about the nature of medical treatment then it is not possible at law for true consent to that treatment to be obtained. Occasionally a doctor will give a brief account of a proposed clinical procedure to a patient leaving it to the nurse to explain in greater detail what is involved. Unless a nurse is sure that she can explain the procedure without misleading the patient she should leave further explanation to the doctor himself.

Who can consent?

Health professionals are sometimes surprised to learn that in English law the only person who can consent to the medical treatment of an adult patient (whether competent or otherwise), is the patient herself. No one else can give legally valid consent on behalf of an adult, even where it appears that the patient lacks capacity. This long established principle has recently been affirmed in the case *Re R (a minor) (wardship medical treatment)*[25] where Lord Donaldson commented that an adult's refusal to give consent is totally effective as a prohibition to treatment, because there is no other person in a position to consent on behalf of an adult.

---

25. *Re R (a minor) (wardship medical treatment)* [1991] 4 All ER 177.

What is the effect of a doctor's failure to provide a patient with sufficient information about the nature of his treatment?

Where a doctor or other health professional fails to give his patient sufficient information to allow her to make a rational decision about her treatment, but nonetheless goes on to treat the patient, he will have treated his patient without her consent. This application of this principle was considered in the case of *Sidaway v Bethlem Royal Hospital* which was discussed at p 26 above.

There are situations however, where a patient's condition is such that as a matter of medical emergency she must be treated although it is impossible for consent to be given; eg the patient may be unconscious, or in so much pain that she is temporarily unable to understand the proposed treatment and to consent to it. In such a case the defence of necessity is available to the doctor.

In *F v West Berkshire Health Authority*[26] Lord Brandon held that the appropriate test to determine whether the defence of necessity should prevail, was to ask whether the treatment was in the best interests of the patient 'if, but only if, it is carried out in order either to save ... lives or to ensure improvement or prevent deterioration in ... physical or mental health'. The *Bolam* test (see p 5 above) was used to determine the patient's best interests; thus if a responsible body of medical opinion believed that it was in the best interests of the patient, treatment would be lawful under the defence of necessity.

This principle was applied in *Re T* (*refusal of medical treatment*) where the court approved the transfusion of blood to a patient who had refused it, on the grounds that due to her illness the patient was not in a position to make a genuine decision as to her treatment. In the absence of either valid consent or valid refusal, the doctors acted out of necessity and in the patient's best interests, in providing the transfusion which was therefore lawful. Lord Donaldson proffered 'Guidance for Doctors and Hospitals' in this case which he later summarised as follows:

- Every adult has the right and capacity to determine whether or not he will accept medical treatment even if a refusal may risk permanent injury to his health or death. However, the presumption of capacity to decide, which stems from the fact the patient is adult, is rebuttable.

- An adult patient may be deprived of his capacity to decide either by long term mental incapacity, or retarded development, or by temporary factors such as unconsciousness or confusion or the effects of fatigue, shock pain or drugs.

---

26. *F v W Berkshire Health Authority* [1990] 2 AC 1.

- If an adult patient does have the capacity to decide at the time of the purported refusal and still does not have that capacity, it is the duty of the doctors to treat him in whatever way they consider, in the exercise of their clinical judgment, to be in his best interests.

- Doctors faced with a refusal of consent have to give very careful and detailed consideration to what was the patient's capacity to decide at the time that the decision was made. It may not be a case of capacity or no capacity. It may be a case of reduced capacity. What matters is whether at that time the patient's capacity was reduced below a level needed in the case of a refusal of that importance, for refusals can vary in importance. Some may involve a risk to life or of irreparable damage to health. Others may not.

- In some cases, doctors will not only have to consider the capacity of the patient to refuse treatment, but also whether the refusal has been vitiated because it resulted not from the patient's will but from the will of others. If his will was overborne, the refusal will not have represented a true decision.

- In all cases doctors will need to consider what is the true scope and basis of the refusal. Was it intended to apply in the circumstances that have arisen? Was it based on assumptions which in the event have not been realised? A refusal is only effective within its true scope, and is vitiated if it is based on false assumptions.

- Forms of refusal should be re-designed to bring the consequences of a refusal forcibly to the attention of patients.

- In cases of doubt as to the effect of a purported refusal of treatment, where failure to treat threatens the patient's life, or threatens irreparable damage to his health, doctors and health authorities should not hesitate to apply to the court for assistance.

This principle was taken further in the case of *Airedale NHS Trust v Bland*[27] where the House of Lords held that where the opinion of a body of competent doctors was that it would not be in the patient's best interests to prolong his life, medical treatment, nutrition and hydration could lawfully be withheld from a patient in a persistent vegetative state with no hope of recovery. Indeed, Lord Browne-Wilkinson was of the opinion that to continue to treat such a patient, for whom there was no hope of recovery, could constitute the tort and crime of trespass to the person.

---

27. *Airedale National Health Service Trust v Bland* [1993] AC 789.

The distinction between explicit and implied consent

Patients who are about to undergo any form of invasive treatment are normally asked to provide written consent to the treatment proposed. The form below is typical of those used by hospitals in such circumstances.

GENERAL CONSENT FORM

I...............................of...

(name & address of person giving consent)

*hereby consent to undergo

OR

*hereby consent to.. undergoing the operation treatment of...the nature and purpose of which has been explained to me by Dr/Mr..

I also consent to such further or alternative operative measures or treatment as may be found necessary during the course of the operation or treatment, and to the administration of general or other anaesthetics for any of these purposes.

No assurance has been given to me that the operation/treatment will be performed/administered by any particular practitioner.

Date...............................

Signature........................

*Patient/parent/guardian

Date...............................

Signature........................

Medical Practitioner

*Delete whichever is inapplicable

The medical profession appears to labour under the naive impression that provided a written consent form has been completed by a patient, no action will lie against those who treat her. A written form of consent has no magic properties, however, unless the patient understands the nature of the proposed treatment and has the capacity to consent to it, the completed consent form will be invalid.

However, in the majority of circumstances where the proposed medical treatment is of a routine nature, a patient's written consent to treatment is not generally sought but may instead be implied from the patient's words or actions. Thus, in a US case (*O'Brien v Cunard*[28]) where an immigrant to the US complained that he had not explicitly consented to a vaccination procedure the

---

28. *O'Brien v Cunard SS Co* (1891) 28 NE 266 (Mass Sup Jud Ct).

court held that by baring his arm and holding it out to the doctor for vaccination he had impliedly consented to the treatment.

Patients incapable of consenting to treatment

Minors

The Children Act 1989 has been seen as a milestone in the protection of children's welfare. Although its provisions are far ranging, however, there is only limited reference to the issue of children, consent and medical treatment.

By s 100, the Act restricts the circumstances under which wardship orders can be granted. Second, under s 44(6)(b) courts are given the power, when making an emergency protection order, to direct that a child be medically or psychiatrically examined but that the child may 'if he is of sufficient understanding to make an informed decision, refuse to submit to the examination or treatment' (s 44). This is the first statutory reference to the right of a competent minor to *refuse* treatment in certain circumstances.

The right of competent minors to *consent* to treatment depends on whether they are over the age of 16 years and thus covered by the provisions of s 8(1) of the Family Law Reform Act 1969. This statute provides that the consent of a minor who has attained the age of 16 years to any surgical, medical or dental treatment 'shall be as effective as it would be if he were of full age'.

Even where a competent minor is under the age of 16 years the ability of such a minor to consent to medical treatment is now established following the case of *Gillick v West Norfolk and Wisbech AHA*[29]. In this case it was held that competent minors can give valid consent to medical treatment even if they are below the age of 16 years providing they have the capacity to understand the proposed treatment. The parental power to consent on behalf of a child diminishes as her powers of understanding increase to the point where she achieves full understanding and acquires the capacity to consent for herself. Lord Scarman stated in his speech in this case:

> I would hold that as a matter of law the parental right to determine whether or not their minor child below the age of 16 will have medical treatment terminates if, and when, the child achieves a sufficient understanding and intelligence to enable him or her to understand fully what is proposed ... it will be a question of fact whether a child ... has sufficient understanding of what is involved to give a consent valid in law.

However, this view has been significantly affected by the more recent decision in *Re R: (a minor) (wardship medical treatment)*[30]. In this case a 15 year old

---

29. *Gillick v West Norfolk and Wisbech Area Health Authority* [1986] AC 112.

30. *Re R (a minor) (wardship: medical treatment)* [1991] 4 All ER 177.

girl, in voluntary care of a local authority, refused to give consent to the medication which was prescribed for her while a patient in an adolescent psychiatric unit. There were two issues at stake. First whether the girl concerned was 'Gillick competent'. Second, whether the court had power to override a minor's refusal to consent to treatment, whether the minor was competent or not, in circumstances where the minor was a ward of court. Lord Donaldson MR in the course of his judgment said that:

> The failure (to consent) or refusal of the Gillick competent child is a very important factor in the doctor's decision whether or not to treat, *but does not prevent the necessary consent being obtained from another competent source* (emphasis added).

Thus following Lord Donaldson's judgment, even where a child is competent, her parents retain a concurrent power to consent. The effect of this decision would appear to be that where a child is Gillick competent she may consent to treatment and this consent cannot be vetoed by her parents. However, her parents still retain the capacity to consent to her being treated, and where they exercise this capacity to consent to treatment on her behalf, the child cannot veto it. This would appear to be inconsistent with the decision in Gillick, and also with some provisions of the Children Act 1989, however, Lord Donaldson's view would now appear to be confirmed by the Court of Appeal in *Re W* (see below).

Further, the Court of Appeal in *Re R* went on to hold that the court, when exercising its wardship jurisdiction, has greater powers than a parent to give or withhold consent, so that, even where the child in question is 'Gillick competent' the court can override that child's decision in circumstances where a natural parent cannot (if following Lord Scarman's view).

In an even more recent case *Re W (a minor) (medical treatment)*[31] a judge authorised the removal of a 16 year old anorexic girl, against her wishes, to a hospital specialising in the treatment of eating disorders. The basis for this decision, which was subsequently approved by the Court of Appeal, was that a court can override the wishes of a mentally competent child, if it appears that it is in a child's best interests to do so (ie where there is the possibility of death or severe permanent injury). The court went on to affirm the decision in *Re R* discussed above, that a competent minor could consent to medical treatment, but this right did not mean that such a child also had an absolute right to refuse treatment where a parent or person exercising parental responsibility, had given consent.

---

31. *Re W (a minor) (medical treatment)* [1992] 4 All ER 627.

The unconscious

Where an unconscious patient is taken to the accident and emergency department of a local hospital, as a result of a road accident, heart attack or other sudden illness, clearly she will not be capable of consenting to the necessary life saving treatment. This does not mean, however, that it would be unlawful for a doctor to treat her, since the defence of necessity will apply in these circumstances provided that it was in the best interest of the patient to treat her in this way.

This defence of necessity based on the concept of the patient's best interests was described in *Re F* by Lord Brandon as follows:

> ... a doctor can lawfully operate on, or give other treatment to, adult patients who are incapable for one reason or another, of consenting to his doing so, provided that the operation or other treatment concerned is in the best interests of such patients. The operation or other treatment will be in their best interests if, but only if, it is carried out either to save their lives, or to ensure improvement or prevent deterioration in their physical or mental health.

Thus, as Lord Goff pointed out in the same case, where an injured passenger is trapped unconscious in the wreckage of a railway accident, it is lawful for a surgeon to amputate a limb to free the passenger from the wreckage, for an ambulance man to convey him to hospital, and for doctors and nurses at the hospital to treat him while he is still unconscious. However, the surgeon should do no more than is reasonably required in the best interests of the patient before he recovers consciousness, when he may then be consulted about long term treatment.

Suppose, however, that in the course of an operation for which the patient has given consent, a surgeon discovers some other medical condition for which the patient, in the doctor's opinion, requires additional medical treatment. In what circumstances may he operate immediately and in what circumstances should he postpone further treatment until the patient has been consulted and given consent; it would appear that the doctor may only act in such a situation if 'a great emergency which could not be anticipated arises (when) ... it is the surgeon's duty to act in order to save the life or preserve the health of the patient' (*Marshall v Curry*[32]).

Adults temporarily or permanently incapable of giving consent

In *Re F* the House of Lords held that where a person was temporarily or permanently incapable of deciding whether to have medical treatment or not, medical intervention could be justified on the basis of the doctrine of necessity, unless it

---

32. *Marshall v Curry* [1933] DLR 260.

conflicted with the known wishes of the patient (see Chapter 8). Thus, treatment of an incompetent adult is lawful if it is in the patient's best interests and if it is directed towards the saving of the patient's life or improvement of his health or well being. Such treatment could range from the removal of a dangerously infected appendix to normal routine dental treatment.

Where the treatment proposed is non-therapeutic however (as for instance in *Re F* the sterilisation of a mentally handicapped adult) this will normally require the prior sanction of a High Court judge. If the incompetent patient is a minor applications to the court should be made within the wardship proceedings in the Family Division of the High Court, which, if the minor is not already a ward, should be commenced for that purpose. The plaintiff or applicant should normally be a parent or those responsible for the care of the patient or those intending to carry out the proposed operation, and the patient's guardian *ad litem* should normally be the Official Solicitor. The purpose of the hearing will be to determine whether the proposed treatment is in fact in the best interests of the patient and that those proposing it are acting in good faith. Medical, psychological and social evaluations of the patient will be presented by experts and the judge will normally require evidence which establishes:

- that the patient is incapable of making his or her own decision;

- that the condition which it is sought to avoid will in fact occur without treatment;

- that the patient will suffer substantial trauma or psychological damage if the condition which it is sought to avoid should arise;

- that there is no practicable alternative means of solving the anticipated problem.

CASE STUDY ONE

Rajiv arrives in theatre having signed a consent form for the debridement of his gangrenous foot. Once in the anaesthetic room the consultant asks Rajiv to consent to amputation of his foot if it appears necessary. Rajiv refuses to consent to amputation.

Some days later Rajiv returns to theatre for the amputation of his foot to which he has by now consented.

Should the consultant on the first occasion have:

- Over-ridden Rajiv's initial refusal and proceeded with the amputation?

- Persuaded the patient to consent?

- Advised and guided the patient towards consent?

- Treated the patient conservatively?

- Discontinued all treatment?

CASE STUDY TWO

Stan is admitted for a prostate resection which is likely to be followed by transfusion. Prior to the operation a blood sample is taken for cross matching, and the patient is asked whether he would be prepared to participate nine months later in an investigation into 'transmissible diseases'. The patient agrees.

Nine months later Stan takes part in the research by donating blood which is then tested for syphilis, hepatitis A & B and HIV.

Has Stan consented to taking part in this experiment?

CASE STUDY THREE

Dennis, a child, is admitted to casualty following a road accident. It is clear to the treating casualty officer that Dennis will die unless a blood transfusion is performed immediately. Dennis' parents, who are Jehovah's Witnesses refuse to consent to the transfusion. Can the doctor lawfully proceed to transfuse the patient with blood products?

3   Compulsory Admission to Hospital under the Mental Health Act 1983

Introduction

The Mental Health Act 1983 and the preceding legislation to the Lunacy Act of 1845 all emerged from a common concern that individuals who are ill or handicapped in ways that render them incapable of autonomous decisions are vulnerable. They need special protection to ensure that their treatment and care is warranted, does not fall below a certain standard of practice and that they are protected from unnecessary or ill treatment[1].

Historically psychiatry has probably been the most controversial area of medicine, primarily because nurses and doctors specialising in the field of psychiatry are called upon to treat patients who are unwilling to receive that treatment, that is, refuse to consent to that treatment. Furthermore, what constitutes 'mental disorder' as opposed, eg to anti-social behaviour is similarly controversial. Indeed, some critics have argued[2] that mental illness does not exist and that psychiatry is used as a means of controlling behaviour which is deemed to be a departure from the accepted norm. In addition there is sometimes disagreement between two psychiatrists who accept the phenomena of mental illness but disagree as to whether a given person is in fact mentally ill. The debate about whether an alleged murderer was 'mad' or 'bad' (that is, whether he was suffering from a mental illness or not) was most vividly illustrated by the Yorkshire Ripper case[3].

The Mental Health Act 1983 makes statutory provision for the compulsory admission to hospital and treatment of the mentally disordered. It is supplemented by a Code of Practice[4] which, although it does not impose either additional statutory duties or a legal obligation to comply with its provisions, a failure to so comply can be referred to in evidence in any legal proceedings pursuant to the Act.

In practice treatment for mental illness is most frequently provided on a voluntary basis (the proportion of voluntary patients has increased very consider-

---

1. E Murphy 'Psychiatry and the Law, Current Approaches' in Duphar (ed) Medical Relations Publications.
2. See, eg T Szasz (1972) *The Myth of Mental Illness*, New York: Harper & Row and R D Laing (1965) *The Divided Self*, Penguin.
3. *R v Sutcliffe* (1981) *The Times* 23 May.
4. Published August 1993 by HMSO to take effect 1 November 1993.

ably over the last 30 years); over 90 per cent of admissions to psychiatric units and hospitals are voluntary admissions.

Informal patients

Section 131 of the Mental Health Act 1983 allows people to enter hospital voluntarily (ie as 'informal patients') for the treatment of mental disorder in the same way as people enter hospital for the treatment of physical disorders.

Informal patients enjoy two legal rights which compulsorily detained patients do not:

• they may leave hospital whenever they like; and

• they may refuse to accept any form of treatment which they do not like (see p 50 below). In addition they have unrestricted access to the courts.

There are, however, circumstances in which informal patients may be compulsorily detained in hospital for up to 72 hours (see p 50 below)

Even though a patient appears willing to enter hospital as a voluntary patient, 'compulsory admission should, however, be considered where the patient's current medical state, together with reliable evidence of past experience, indicates a strong likelihood that he will change his mind about informal admission prior to his actual admission to hospital with a resulting risk to his health or safety or to the safety of others'[5].

Compulsorily detained patients

There are three ways in which a person may be admitted to a hospital as a detained patient under the provisions of the Mental Health Act 1983:

• following an application by an 'approved social worker' or by the patient's nearest relative, supported by medical recommendations (Part II);

• by order of a criminal court (Part III);

• on transfer from prison by Home Office warrant (Part III).

Applications under Part II

Part II governs compulsory admission for assessment and treatment as well as making provision for application for guardianship. Compulsory admission clearly has important implications for civil liberties and the legislation is drafted

---

5. Code of Practice p 5.

to ensure that compulsory detention is only lawful if the person so detained is adjudged to be suffering from an illness as opposed to merely displaying non-conformist behaviour. The Code of Practice requires health care professionals involved in assessing patients for possible compulsory admission to ensure that all the relevant factors are taken into account, that possible appropriate alternatives to compulsory admission are considered, and that the legal requirements of the Act are complied with.

Admission for assessment

Section 2 allows an application for admission (by an approved social worker or nearest relative who must have seen the person within the preceding 14 days) for assessment and authorises detention for up to 28 days. The application must be supported by a recommendation from two doctors, one an approved specialist in mental disorder, to the effect that:

- the patient 'is suffering from mental disorder of a nature or degree which warrants the detention of the patient for assessment (or assessment followed by medical treatment) for at least a limited period; and

- he ought to be so detained in the interests of his own health or safety or the safety of other persons'.

Thus two conditions must be satisfied, the patient must be suffering from a mental disorder, and one of the conditions under the second head above must apply. Before application for compulsory admission is made, consideration must be given to whether the patient would be willing to accept medical treatment informally or as an out-patient.

An 'approved social worker' (ASW) is a social worker approved by a local social service authority as 'having appropriate competence in dealing with persons who are suffering from a mental disorder' (Mental Health Act, s 114). The ASW has overall responsibility for co-ordinating the patient's assessment and, where he decides to make an application for admission, for implementing that decision. He must also attempt to identify the patient's 'nearest relative' (s 26) and take such steps as are practicable to inform the nearest relative about an application for admission under s 2 and his power of discharge (s 11(2)).

A 'nearest relative' is the first person on the list below who is surviving:

- husband or wife;

- son or daughter;

- father or mother;

- brother or sister;

- grandparent;

- grandchild;

- uncle or aunt;

- nephew or niece.

Whole blood relatives are preferred to half blood and eldest rather than youngest, regardless of sex (Mental Health Act, s 26).

The court has power to appoint a nearest relative (Mental Health Act, s 29) where there is no nearest relative, or where the nearest relative is incapable of acting or unreasonably objects to making application for compulsory admission, or where the nearest relative has exercised his power to discharge the patient without due regard either to his welfare or the interests of the public on the application of any relative of the patient, any other person with whom the patient is residing, or an approved social worker.

Definition of mental disorder

Section 1(2) defines 'mental disorder' as 'mental illness, arrested or incomplete development of mind, psychopathic disorder and any other disorder or disability of mind'. 'Mental illness' is not defined (the difficulties in this area have been referred to above) although s 1(2) does provide a definition of 'mental impairment', 'severe mental impairment' and 'psychopathic disorder'. Section 1(3) does, however, provide that a person cannot be dealt with under the Act as suffering from mental disorder or from any specific form of it, 'by reason only of promiscuity or other immoral conduct, sexual deviancy or dependence on alcohol or drugs'.

Duty of hospital managers

Section 132 places on the hospital manager the duty to inform both the detained patient and her nearest relative (unless the patient refuses) of her rights under the Mental Health Act (eg the right to appeal to a Mental Health Review Tribunal). The information must be provided both orally and in writing. Section 133 requires, in the absence of the patient objecting, that the nearest relative be given (if practicable) at least seven days' notice of a detained patient's discharge, especially if that relative is to be involved in the aftercare of the patient.

Compulsory treatment of s 2 patients

Although s 2 seems primarily to be concerned with 'assessment' rather than 'treatment' and it is clear that admission for medical treatment alone would be unlawful under s 2, treatment may legitimately follow an initial assessment.

Thus most forms of treatment for mental disorder can be given without consent subject to the provisos in ss 57 and 58 (see p 52 below).

Discharge of patients detained under s 2

A person detained under s 2 has the right to apply for discharge to a Mental Health Review Tribunal (MHRT) within 14 days of admission who may discharge the patient. It seems, however, that a patient detained under s 2 who is ordered to be discharged by a Mental Health Review Tribunal in pursuance of its powers under the Mental Health Act s 72 may, if the conditions in s 3 are satisfied, be compulsorily detained under that section even before the MHRT's discharge order has taken effect (*R v Managers of South Western hospital and another ex p M*[6]).

The responsible medical officer (RMO) or the hospital authorities or the nearest relative may also discharge the patient within the 28 day detention period (s 23)). On expiry of the 28 day period the patient cannot continue to be detained by effecting another s 2 order. The patient may agree to stay voluntarily or could be made the subject of a compulsory treatment order under s 3 (below).

Admission for treatment

Section 3 of the Mental Health Act provides that an application for admission for treatment may be made by either the nearest relative or a social worker. If the nearest relative objects to admission on these grounds the social worker must apply to the county court for authority. The detention in the first instance is for six months and may be renewed for a further six months and thereafter from year to year. The recommendation must be supported by two doctors, one an approved specialist to the effect that the patient is suffering from a mental disorder of such nature or degree that hospital treatment is necessary for the health or safety of the patient or for the protection of other people and that treatment cannot be provided unless detention under this section is effected.

Conditions justifying compulsory admission for treatment

Compulsory admission under s 3 is more closely controlled than under s 2 (above). A patient may openly be compulsorily detained if she is suffering from one of the following four identifiable mental disorders:

- mental illness;

- severe mental impairment;

---

6. *R v Managers of South Western hospital and another ex p M* [1986] QB 1090.

- psychopathic disorder; or

- mental impairment.

Patients suffering from either mental illness or severe mental impairment may be admitted under s 3 irrespective of whether they are likely to benefit from the treatment. Patients who are diagnosed as suffering from either psychopathic disorder or mental impairment may only be detained if they are likely to benefit from the treatment.

Treatment under s 3

The treatability test does not, of course, entail any undertaking that treatment will effect a cure for the patient so detained, the treatment must simply be 'likely to alleviate or prevent a deterioration of his condition' (s 3(2)(b)). Given that the compulsory detention is to effect some form of treatment most forms may be given without consent (subject to the provisos in ss 56-57 see p 52 below).

Treatment of psychopaths has long been a problem for the psychiatric profession. Psychopathy (that is 'a persistent disorder or disability of mind (whether or not including significant impairment of intelligence) which results in abnormally aggressive or seriously irresponsible conduct on the part of the person concerned' s 1(2)) is regarded now as being potentially treatable at least. Patients may be detained under s 3 (*R v Mersey Mental Health Review Tribunal ex p D*[7]) even if there is no specific therapy available as the Mental Health Act s 72, which deals with the powers of Mental Health Review tribunals to order the discharge of detained patients, defines 'treatment' as including nursing, care and rehabilitation.

On an application by the RMO to renew a s 3 detention order the RMO must believe that further treatment is likely to alleviate or prevent deterioration in the patient's condition or that the patient would be unable to care for herself or would be liable to serious exploitation if the detention ended (s 20(4)(a)).

Section 3 is not available to force treatment on non-consenting out-patients. In *R v Hallstrom, ex p W*[8] the courts made it clear that it is unlawful to admit a person under s 3 with the intention of, eg, administering a long-acting tranquillising injection, and then immediately discharging the patient back into the community. Following a series of much publicised violent (sometimes fatal) attacks made by psychiatric patients while being cared for in the community suggestions have been made that the compulsory treatment provisions be extended to such patients. Section 117 does, however, require health authorities

---

7. *R v Mersey Mental Health Tribunal ex p D* (1987) *The Times*, 13 April.

8. *R v Hallstrom, ex p W* [1993] 3 WLR 376.

and local authorities, in conjunction with voluntary agencies, to provide after-care for discharged psychiatric patients.

Discharge of s 3 patients

The RMO can order the discharge of a patient detained under s 3 before the expiry of the six month period as may the hospital managers and the nearest relative (s 23(2)(a)). In addition the patient may make application for discharge to a MHRT within the first six months, within the second six months and there-after annually. An automatic referral (by the hospital manager) is made to the MHRT in the second six month period (ie the patient need not instigate this) and thereafter every three years.

Emergency detention orders

Section 4 allows an application (by nearest relative or social worker) for admission for assessment in an emergency with the support of only one medical recommendation (the doctor need not be 'approved'). The grounds are the same as in s 2 but both the applicant and doctor must certify that 'it is of urgent necessity for the patient to be admitted and detained' and that compliance with s 2 'would involve undesirable delay'.

Detention is authorised for up to 72 hours but may be converted into a s 2 admission by the provision of a second medical recommendation within that time.

While a patient is detained within the provisions of s 4 no treatment can be administered without the patient's consent but neither does that patient have access to a Mental Health Review Tribunal.

Detention of an informal patient

An informal patient may be detained in hospital compulsorily in the following circumstances:

- Where the doctor in charge of the patient's treatment furnishes a report to the hospital managers to the effect that 'it appears that an application ought to be made' (Mental Health Act, s 5). Detention in these circumstances is for up to 72 hours. The patient must not already be the subject of a compulsory detention order under the Mental Health Act and need not be receiving treatment for a mental disorder; treatment for a physical illness is sufficient.

The health authority, NHS trust or local authority social services department has a responsibility to ensure that the patient is fully assessed as quickly as possible by an ASW and two doctors for possible admission under the Act.

Section 132 requires the hospital manager to provide the patient with information about the implications of her detention.

- Where a registered first level nurse trained in the care of the mentally ill or mentally handicapped believes that the patient is suffering from mental disorder to such a degree that detention is necessary for his health or safety or the protection of others (s 5(4)). Detention is up to six hours or until the earlier arrival of a doctor. The decision of the relevant nurse is a personal one and no one else has the power to instruct him to use it.

Patients detained under s 5 cannot be given treatment without their consent but there is no facility for such a detained patient to apply to the Mental Health Review Tribunal for discharge.

Place of safety orders

Section 136 provides a police officer with the right to take a person to a 'place of safety' for up to 72 hours where he finds a person in a public place who appears to him to be suffering from a mental disorder and in need of care or control.

There is no power to impose medical treatment without the consent of the patient so detained but neither does that patient have the right to apply to a Mental Health Review Tribunal for discharge.

Criminal courts and compulsory detention under Part III

Under s 37 a criminal court may make a hospital order in relation to certain criminal offenders. The effect of s 37 is comparable to that of s 3, so that the patient's fate is controlled by the medical authorities rather than the court. The order lasts for six months and can be renewed after six months and then annually.

The court has power to use s 37 when it is satisfied on the written or oral evidence of two registered medical practitioners that the offender is suffering from mental disorder, that detention in hospital is appropriate, and that, given the nature of the offence this is 'the most suitable method of disposing of the case'.

The person must be guilty of an imprisonable offence other than murder.

The detention may be challenged in a MHRT within the second six months of detention and thereafter annually.

Automatic referral is made to the MHRT after the second six months and thereafter every three years.

Under s 41 the Crown Court may make a restriction order if, in addition to the grounds for making an order within s 37 (above) it 'appears to the court, having regard to the nature of the offence, the antecedents of the offender and the risk of him committing further offences if set at large, that it is necessary for the protection of the public from serious harm'.

Application can be made to a MHRT within the second six months of detention and thereafter annually. MHRT's are mandatorily obliged to discharge a patient in the following circumstances:

- if the patient is not suffering from a mental illness;

- if the disorder suffered is not appropriate for detention in hospital;

- it is not necessary for the public safety.

Automatic referral is made every three years.

If a patient on a restriction order is conditionally discharged he can be recalled on order of the Secretary of State at any time. However, the patient must have access to a MHRT within one month of recall.

Section 36 gives the Crown Court power to remand to hospital for treatment where it has evidence from two doctors (one 'approved') that the person is suffering from mental illness or severe mental impairment.

Transfer from prison by Home Office Warrant

Sections 47 and 48 empower the Home Secretary to direct the transfer to hospital of remand prisoners and those serving custodial sentences. Remand prisoners must be the subject of a restriction order. The Home Secretary has discretion in other cases as to whether to make the patient subject to a restriction order or not.

If a patient is detained unlawfully then he may seek damages for false imprisonment. If the Mental Health Act has been properly complied with, detention will not usually be unlawful. An originally lawful detention will be unlawful if a patient is detained in conditions which are 'so seriously prejudicial to her health' (*Furber v Kratter*[9]).

In *Knight v Home Office*[10] it was held that the appropriate standard of care for mentally ill prisoners detained in a prison hospital is not as high as that in a psychiatric hospital.

Mental patients' access to the courts

Section 139(1) provides that people will not be liable for actions purported to be carried out in pursuance of the provisions of the Act unless 'the act was done in bad faith or without reasonable care'.

---

9. *Furber v Kratter* (1988) *The Times* 21 July.

10. *Knight v Home Office* (1990) *Independent* 24 January.

This is no protection against liability in negligence but it does protect against honest and reasonable mistakes, including a mistake about the extent of their powers.

Section 139(2) provides that, in order to sue in respect of acts covered by s 139(1) the patient must have leave of the High Court.

In *Poutney v Griffiths*[11] it was held that the actions of a Broadmoor nurse which he claimed were done to control a detained patient were 'acts purporting to be in pursuance of the Act'.

The treatment of informal patients is not within the provisions of s 139 (*R v Moonsami Runighian*[12]).

Section 139 does not apply to applications for judicial review to quash allegedly illegal admissions (*ex p Waldron*[13]).

Medical treatment for patients detained under the Mental Health Act 1983

The Mental Health Act 1959 was based upon the presumption that involuntary mental patients were not competent to consent to medical treatment. In 1979 however, the European Court of Human Rights held that this presumption was in conflict with Article 6 of the European Convention on Human Rights and it was, in part, as a result of this decision, that the Mental Health Act 1983 was enacted. The fundamental principle on which this is based is that just as any other patient must give consent if treatment is to be lawful, so too must a mental patient, subject to certain exceptions.

Voluntary patients and those detained for a period of no longer than 72 hours

Voluntary patients (ie those for whom no statutory provisions are used to secure their presence in the hospital) are in exactly the same position as any other patients at common law in relation to the giving of, and the withholding of, consent to treatment.

Patients detained in hospital by a doctor for up to 72 hours (s 5(2)), by a registered mental nurse for up to six hours (s 5(4)) or for emergency assessment (s 4) are also governed by the common law.

---

11. *Poutney v Griffiths* [1976] AC 314.

12. *R v Moonsami Runighian* [1977] Crim LR 361.

13. *ex p Waldron* [1986] QB 824.

Compulsorily detained patients

Where patients are detained for a longer term under the provisions of the Mental Health Act, consent to treatment is governed by Part IV of that Act. This provides that medical treatment for the mental disorder from which the patient is suffering (but not for physical illness or any other condition: see *Re F (sterilisation of incompetent patient)*[14]) may be given to a patient who either refuses to consent or is incompetent to do so (s 63). Part IV, however, contains certain important safeguards. Thus some treatments require either the patient's consent and/or a second opinion.

The administration of medication beyond a three month period

Medication for mental disorder may be given without consent to a patient compulsorily detained under the Mental Health Act 1983. The administration of medication beyond that three month time limit is subject either to the patient consenting or the obtaining of a second opinion via the Mental Health Act Commission (s 58). This three month period gives time for the doctor to create a treatment programme suitable for the patient's needs; although the patient may be treated without consent during this period, no such treatment should be given in the absence of an attempt to obtain voluntary consent. If medication in likely to be given beyond the three month period the Code of Practice suggests that the need for consent should be foreseen in good time and the appropriate action taken.

Code of Practice

The Code of Practice published in August 1993 pursuant to the Mental Health Act 1983, s 118 defines 'consent' as the voluntary and continuing permission of the patient to receive a particular treatment, based on an adequate knowledge of the purpose, nature, likely effects and risks of that treatment including the likelihood of its success and any alternatives to it. Permission given under any unfair or undue pressure is not 'consent'.

The Code states that the assessment of a patient's capacity to make a decision about his own medical treatment should be a matter for clinical judgment, guided by current professional practice and subject to any relevant legal requirements.

The basic principles of capacity are described in the Code as follows. In order to have capacity, an individual must be able to:

- understand what medical treatment is and that somebody has said that he needs it and why the treatment is being proposed;

---

14. *sterilisation of incompetent patient* [1990] 2 AC 1.

- understand in broad terms the nature of the treatment proposed;

- understand its principal benefits and risks;

- understand what the consequences of not receiving the proposed treatment will be;

- possess the capacity to make a choice.

The Code also requires that any assessment as to an individual's capacity has to be made in relation to a specific treatment proposal and that it must be remembered that capacity can vary over time and should only be assessed at the time that treatment is proposed; there is also a requirement that the patient's notes should fully record all assessments of a patient's capacity.

Electro convulsive therapy

If a responsible medical officer proposes to administer ECT a valid consent from the patient should always be sought. If the consent is not forthcoming (s 58) a second opinion must be obtained. The Second Opinion Appointed Doctor (who is appointed by the Mental Health Act Commission), must indicate, if in his opinion ECT is indicated, the proposed number of applications.

Psychosurgery treatment requiring consent and a second opinion

Treatment involving psychosurgery requires the patient's consent and other special procedures must be followed as defined in the Mental Health Act, s 57(1)(a). Psychosurgery is defined by the Act as 'any surgical operation for destroying brain tissue or for destroying the function of brain tissue'. Subsequent Regulations have added to this definition 'the surgical implantation of hormones to reduce the male sex drive'. The Code of Practice emphasises that the implantation of hormones to reduce male sexual drive is only covered by s 57 where it is administered as a medical treatment for a mental disorder.

By s 57(2)(a) of the Act psychosurgery cannot be given unless:

(a) the patient consents; and

(b) a registered medical practitioner appointed for this purpose by the Secretary of State (not being the responsible medical officer) and two other persons appointed by the Secretary of State certify in writing that the patient is capable of understanding the nature purpose and likely effects of the treatment and has consented to it; and

(c) the registered doctor referred to in (b) above has certified that having regard to the likelihood of treatment alleviating or preventing a deterioration in the patient's condition the treatment should be given;

(d) the registered doctor referred to in (b) above consults two other persons who have been professionally concerned with the patient's medical treatment (one of whom must be a nurse and the other of whom may be neither a nurse nor a doctor).

The limitations of the application of s 57 are amply demonstrated by the case of *R v Mental Health Appeals Commissioners ex p W*[15]; here the court was required to interpret the meaning of 'the surgical implantation of hormones' in relation to the injection of a capsule containing the drug goserelin (Zoladex ICI) which acts as a block to the hormone message system. This drug was given, with W's consent, to prevent his sexual urges which had in the past led him to attack young children. On the basis that the treatment was for a mental disorder (and this is debateable), the court held that:

- the substance was not a hormone (but a hormone analogue); and

- the injection of the implant was not a 'surgical procedure'; thus its administration did not fall under the provisions of s 57, but rather under the provisions of s 63 for the first three months, and thereafter under the provisions of s 58; and

- the Mental Health Act Commission had applied too stringent a test when deciding the issue of the patient's competence to consent to the treatment. 'I cannot accept that a patient must understand the precise physiological process involved before he can be said to be capable of understanding the nature and likely effects of the treatment and can consent to it' *per* Stuart Smith LJ.

Withdrawal of consent under s 60

If a patient has consented to treatment as required by ss 57 and 58 of the Act she may at any time before or during the course of treatment, withdraw that consent. No further treatment may then be undertaken without the provisions of ss 57 and 58 being again complied with. These provisions are subject to the provisions for urgent treatment (s 62) outlined below.

Urgent treatment under s 62

The need to follow the procedures under ss 57 and 58 may be avoided where a patient requires emergency treatment, providing that the conditions in s 62 are satisfied, ie that the treatment:

- is immediately necessary to save the patient's life; or

---

15. *R v Mental Health Appeals Commissioners ex p W* (1988) *The Times* 27 May.

- not being irreversible, is immediately necessary to prevent a serious deterioration in his condition; or

- not being irreversible or hazardous is immediately necessary to alleviate serious suffering by the patient; or

- not being irreversible or hazardous, is immediately necessary and represents the minimum interference necessary to prevent the patient from behaving violently or being a danger to himself or others.

Hospitals should ensure that a form is devised to be completed by the patient's RMO every time urgent treatment is given under s 62. Such a form should require details to be given of the proposed treatment; why it is of urgent necessity to give the treatment; and the length of time for which the treatment was given. Note that there is no authority under the Mental Health Act for the compulsory treatment of a patient who is not detained in hospital[16].

Treatment for a physical disorder

Where patients are detained in a mental hospital under the Mental Health Act and require treatment for a physical disorder, the situation is covered not by the Mental Health Act but by the common law. An excellent example of the operation of this principle can be found in the case of *Re C*[17].

C was a long term Broadmoor patient suffering from schizophrenia, who was diagnosed in September 1993 as having gangrene in his right foot. Medical staff believed that C would die unless his right leg were amputated below the knee, and that his chances of survival with 'conservative' treatment would be less than 15 per cent.

C refused his consent to the amputation and his leg was 'conservatively' treated, as a result of which the 85 per cent chance of death was averted. However, the hospital refused to give an undertaking that it would not carry out the amputation at some time in the future should the patient's condition deteriorate.

C therefore asked the court to exercise its inherent jurisdiction to rule, by way of an injunction, that the hospital could not amputate his right leg, without his express written consent.

Mr Justice Thorpe, in considering the application, held that the question to be determined was whether the presumption that C had the right of self determination should be rebutted, on the grounds that his mental capacity was so reduced by his chronic illness, that he did not understand the nature, purpose and effects of the proposed treatment. The court held that although the patient's

---

16. *R v Halstrom, ex p W* [1993] 3 WLR 376.

17. *Re C* [1994] 1 All ER 819.

general capacity was undoubtedly impaired by his illness, it had not been satis-factorily established that C did not understand the nature purpose and effect of the proposed treatment. On this basis the injunction was granted.

Role of the Mental Health Act Commission

The Mental Health Act Commission (MHAC) was established by s 121 Mental Health Act 1983 to provide a variety of functions. It acts as a forum to hear and investigate patients' complaints. All compulsarily detained patients should be informed of their right to complain to the MHAC and the Code of Practice requires staff to provide reasonable assistance to formulate complaints where patients are unable to do so themselves. Leaflets explaining the work and membership of the MHAC should be available to patients or reference made to their availability in hospital admission booklets.

The MHAC also appoints 'Second Opinion Appointed Doctors' who are required to carry out various functions under the Act (for example, the operation of s 57, p 52 above). When a patient has been treated under s 57 or s 58 a review by the MHAC on behalf of the Secretary of State must take place.

CASE STUDY ONE

Mrs Andrews is suffering from Alzheimer's disease. She lives alone but is increasingly becoming vulnerable. She is not eating regularly, her house is dirty and she is of unkempt appearance. Furthermore, she has refused all help from the social services department. Her general practitioner, Dr Bond, is anxious about her, but is assured by her relatives (she has a son who lives nearby and a daughter who lives 50 miles away) that they will look after her. Dr Bond subsequently discovers that the promises made by the son and daughter have not been fulfilled. Dr Bond is becoming increasingly anxious about Mrs Andrews.

Advise Dr Bond of the steps he might consider taking.

CASE STUDY TWO

Paul is aged 74 years and suffers from manic depressive psychosis (a bipolar illness giving rise to violent swings of mood which range from withdrawn and suicidal behaviour to sexually disturbed and very talkative behaviour).

In the manic stage of his illness, Paul is violent to hospital staff and to visitors. Dr James treats Paul with lithium carbonate, but to no effect. He then suggests ECT treatment but Paul refuses to consent to this treatment on the grounds that following previous ECT treatment he had suffered from violent headaches.

Dr James then prescribes thioridazine (Melaril) 400 mg daily 'until he is drowsy enough to consent to ECT'. Paul becomes drowsy, with slurred speech and suffers from incontinence and postural hypotension. He appears to give his consent and receives ECT treatment.

Did Dr James act lawfully in treating Paul?

4 Medical Treatment and the Criminal Law

Introduction

According to the Confidential Enquiry into Perioperative Deaths of 1987 about 1,000 people die every year following medical treatment. In such circumstances there has always been the possibility that medical staff may be named as defendants in civil litigation; in addition they may be involved in hospital complaints and/or GMC disciplinary procedures. There is also now an increasing possibility that they may be charged with a criminal offence.

Murder

English law does not have a single offence of homicide but is divided into the offences of murder and manslaughter. Murder, the more serious offence, is committed where a patient dies as a result of an act which the defendant intended to cause death or grievous bodily harm. This offence is only rarely relevant in the area of medical law, although the recent case of *Beverly Allitt* is a sad exception to this principle.

It is well established that the unlawful killing of any human being with malice aforethought constitutes the crime of murder, whatever the motive of the defendant. This principle was applied in the well known case of *Arthur*[1] where the defendant was charged with the murder of a baby for whom Dr Arthur had prescribed non-treatment and appetite suppressing drugs, because he believed that it was more humane to allow the child, severely handicapped as it was, to die rather than to treat it. In this case, the judge directed the jury that Dr Arthur's motive was irrelevant providing that he had the necessary *mens rea* (guilty mind) and *actus reus* (guilty act) to constitute the offence.

Similarly in the famous case of *Dr Bodkin Adams*[2] Devlin J directed the jury that it did not matter that the patient's death was inevitable and that her days were numbered if it was the intention of the defendant that she should die:

> ... if her life were cut short by weeks or months, it was just as much murder as if it were cut short by years. The law knows no special defence by which doctors might be justified in administering drugs which would shorten life in cases of severe pain, but that did not mean that a doctor who was aiding the sick and dying had to calculate in minutes or even in

1. *R v Arthur* (1981) 12 BMLR 1.
2. *R v Bodkin Adams* [1957] Crim LR 365.

hours and perhaps not in days or weeks, the effect upon a patient's life of the medicines he administers or else be in peril of a charge of murder.

Thus if the first purpose of medicine, ie the restoring of a patient to health, cannot be achieved, there is still a role for the doctor, who is entitled to do all he can to alleviate a patient's suffering, even if of necessity his treatment shortens the patient's life. It would appear therefore that if a patient dies as a result of the effect of pain relieving drugs, administered with the sole purpose of relieving suffering, then in law the doctor's action will not have been the cause of death, but rather the illness from which the patient suffered. On the other hand, if the sole purpose of the administration of drugs is to bring the patient's life to an end, then provided the legal requirements of *mens rea* and *actus reus* are fulfilled, the criminal offence of murder will have been committed.

Mens rea

Following the decision of the Court of Appeal in *Nedrick*[3] in which the *mens rea* for murder was redefined, a court must now ask whether a doctor actually foresaw that there was a risk of death which would arise as a natural and highly probable consequence of his act.

If the jury are satisfied that at the material time the defendant recognised that death (or serious harm) would be virtually certain (barring some unforeseen intervention) to result from his voluntary act, then that is a fact from which they may find it easy to infer that he intended to kill (or do serious bodily harm) even though he may not have had any desire to achieve that result.

It was on this basis that Dr Cox[4] was convicted of (attempted) murder in 1993. It was alleged that he had deliberately injected intravenously two ampoules of undiluted potassium chloride into his elderly patient Lilian Boyes, not for therapeutic purpose, but rather with the intention of causing her immediate death. As a result of the injection the patient died within a space of about one minute.

The judge directed the jury that they must decide whether Dr Cox's primary purpose in administering the drug was to hasten her death or to alleviate her suffering. If (as the jury subsequently found) the intention was primarily to hasten death, then Dr Cox had the necessary *mens rea* and was found guilty of attempted murder. Readers may be puzzled by the fact that Dr Cox was convicted of attempted murder rather than murder, since the patient undoubtedly died as a result of the treatment that was administered. The legal reason for this decision was that Mrs Boyes was suffering from a terminal illness, and it could not be proved, beyond all reasonable doubt, as the criminal law requires, that it

---

3. *R v Nedrick* [1986] 1 WLR 1025.
4. *R v Cox* (1992) 12 BMLR 38.

was the injection of potassium chloride that had killed her rather than her serious illness.

Actus reus

The criminal law does not punish people for evil thoughts or intentions, they must also bring about the act prohibited by the law. Thus once the necessary *mens rea* is established, the next question is whether the act of the doctor amounts to a sufficient *actus reus* (guilty act) for the purposes of the criminal law. In most cases this will amount to a voluntary act on the part of the defendant, such as the act of Dr Cox in administering the lethal injection to his patient.

Where a doctor has merely omitted to act, and it is this omission that is alleged to have brought about the death of his patient, the general rule of criminal law is that the doctor will only be liable where it can be shown that he had a positive duty to act which arose from an earlier assumption of care to the patient. This principle can give rise to criminal liability where a doctor or other health professionals discontinue treatment to a terminally ill patient.

This issue was comprehensively dealt with by the House of Lords in the case of *Airedale HA v Bland*[5]. In this case an application was made by the Airedale HA for a declaration that it was lawful for doctors to withdraw life supporting medical treatment, including artificial feeding by nasogastric tube, from a patient who was in a persistent vegetative state with no prospect of recovery or improvement, when it was known that the discontinuation of treatment would cause his death within a few weeks. A doctor who acted in this way would have the necessary mens rea for murder since he would undoubtedly intend that as a result of his omission the patient should die. An issue for the court in this case was whether such an omission could amount to the necessary *actus reus* for murder.

The first point to be decided was whether or not providing nutrition and hydration amounted to 'medical treatment' or simply nursing care. The earlier US case of *Barber v Supreme Court*[6] had decided that the provision of nutrition and hydration did amount to medical treatment on the grounds that it was more similar to other forms of medical treatment than to normal 'human ways of providing nutrition and hydration'. Thus it was argued, just as a respirator may be medically necessary when lung function is impaired, and a dialysis machine may be required when the kidneys fail, similarly medical nutrition may become necessary because of trauma or disease affecting the alimentary system. In each of these examples mechanical devices perform vital bodily func-

---

5.   *Airedale HA v Bland* [1993] 2 WLR 316.

6.   *Barber v Supreme Court* (1983) 195 Calif Rptr 484.

tions and prolong life, thus being defined as medical treatment. The later case of *Cruzan v The Supreme Court of the US*[7] had confirmed that, in the US at least, the supply of nutrition and hydration undoubtedly amounts to medical treatment. In *Bland* the House of Lords agreed with this view.

The next point for consideration was whether the ending of this medical treatment amounted to an act or to an omission. This was a very important distinction since (as explained above) in English criminal law there is only limited liability for omissions to act (ie where there is a duty to act (see eg *R v Stone and Dobinson*[8]). In *Cruzan* it had been decided held that the withdrawal of nutrition amounted to an omission but that this was non culpable because the doctor had no duty to act in such circumstances. Kennedy[9] has criticised this approach on the grounds that 'it does some considerable violence to ordinary English usage'. What he means by this is that positive acts are undoubtedly required in order to bring about the cessation of treatment: thus the nasogastric tube must be disconnected and physically removed from the patient, and it seems rather strange to describe such acts as omissions to act.

However, the House of Lords, following these US decisions, held that the discontinuation of treatment would amount to an omission, and that such an omission to act by a doctor would not be criminal because it would not be in breach of the doctor's duty to the patient. Lord Goff (who gave the leading speech in this case) stated that such an omission would not amount to a criminal breach of duty because although the sanctity of human life was a fundamental principle, this principle was not absolute and there was no absolute rule that a patient's life had to be prolonged at all costs. Where a patient was incapable of communicating and had given no earlier indication as to his wishes there was no absolute obligation upon the doctor to prolong his life regardless of circumstances.

Lord Goff (in *Airedale HA v Bland*) explained the distinction between 'the doctor who gives his patient a lethal injection which kills him' and 'the doctor who, by discontinuing life support, allows his patient to die'.

In the first case the doctor is guilty of murder; in the second case he is not because 'what the doctor does when he switches off a life support machine is not an act but an omission to struggle' and this omission is not a breach of duty by the doctor because 'he is not obliged to struggle in a hopeless case'.

---

7. *Cruzan v The Supreme Court of the US* (1990) 110 S Ct 2841.

8. *R v Stone and Dobinson* [1977] 2 All ER 341.

9. Kennedy & Grubb (1994) *Medical Law: Text with Materials* p 1210, Butterworths.

Manslaughter

Manslaughter, the less serious homicide offence, is sub-divided into:

- offences under the Homicide Act 1957 (intentional killing in response to provocation, intentional killing where the defendant was suffering from diminished responsibility, and intentional killing in pursuance of a suicide pact); and

- involuntary manslaughter which is in turn subdivided into:

(a) unlawful act manslaughter (where a victim dies as a result of a dangerous and unlawful act intentionally committed); and

(b) gross negligence (or reckless) manslaughter, where a defendant commits a lawful act with such recklessness or negligence as to incur criminal liability.

For the purposes of this book, the area which is of prime concern to health professionals is that of gross negligence (or reckless) manslaughter as defined in (b) above.

In the past it was very rare for health professionals to be charged with manslaughter, following the death of a patient under their care, although it is true that the leading case on gross negligence manslaughter did in fact concern a doctor (*Bateman*[10]).

In this case a doctor performing a manual version during childbirth, mistakenly removed a portion of the patient's uterus, ruptured her bladder and crushed her colon against the sacral promontory; predictably, the patient died seven days later and Dr Bateman was charged with manslaughter. He was initially convicted, but subsequently and perhaps surprisingly given the facts, acquitted on appeal.

The expression 'gross negligence' manslaughter proved difficult to interpret and it began to appear that it had been replaced by the term 'reckless manslaughter' where the expression 'reckless' was interpreted following Lord Diplock's model direction on recklessness in *Caldwell*[11]. However, this view now seems premature in the light of two more recent cases[12] where it would appear that the term 'gross negligence' manslaughter is still the appropriate one where health professionals are concerned.

Since 1990 at least three doctors (all anaesthetists) have been charged with

---

10. *R v Bateman* [1925] 94 LJKB, CC.

11. *R v Caldwell* [1982] AC 341. See eg *R v Seymour* [1983] 2 AC.

12. *R v Ball* (1990) 90 Cr App Rep 378 and *R v Prentice and Sullman* (1993) NLJ 850.

manslaughter; in two of these cases the defendants were convicted[13] while in the third case charges against the defendant who was a registrar at Lister General Hospital were dropped at trial when the medical experts for the prosecution changed their evidence at the last minute. These cases was followed in 1991 by the prosecution of two junior hospital doctors (Doctors Prentice and Sullman) for manslaughter, following the death of a 16 year old leukemia patient (*R v Prentice and Sullman*[14]).

In this case Dr Prentice (a pre-registration houseman) was asked by his registrar to administer Methotrexate and Vincristine to a young leukemia patient who attended regularly for such treatment. Dr Prentice then asked for supervision in performing the lumbar puncture as he had never carried one out before. A more senior colleague Dr Sullman, who was a houseman and had had one (unsuccessful) experience of performing a lumbar puncture, agreed to supervise this procedure. Dr Prentice performed the lumbar puncture successfully and then, without checking the labels on the syringes and the boxes in which they were contained, mistakenly injected the patient intrathecally with both drugs. Thus it was that Vincristine was injected into the patient's spine (rather than intravenously) with inevitable and fatal results.

Dr Prentice claimed that he had believed that both the initial lumbar puncture and the administration of the drugs were being supervised by Dr Sullman. However it appears that an 'important and regrettable misunderstanding took place' for Dr Sullman thought that he was only present to supervise the use of the needle to make a lumbar puncture and had no responsibility over the administration of the cytotoxic drugs.

The case against Dr Prentice was that his behaviour was reckless since he ought to have known of the dangers involved in an intrathecal injection of Vincristine, and he ought to have checked the labels on the syringes and on the boxes in which they were stored before injecting the drugs. (These labels indicated the name of the patient the name of the drug and the route by which it was to be injected.) Because Dr Prentice failed to carry out these procedures the fatal mistake was made and the trial court found that he had acted recklessly and accordingly convicted him of manslaughter.

The case against Dr Sullman was that he too was reckless since he had a duty to supervise the whole operation and to ensure that the right drugs were injected at the right place by checking the labels and making sure that Dr Prentice injected the drugs correctly. Alternatively it was argued that he was reckless in not intervening when he saw that Dr Prentice was preparing to inject the patient with a drug, without having checked the labels. The trial court also found that Dr Sullman had acted recklessly and he too was convicted of manslaughter.

---

13. *R v Sergeant* (1990) *The Lancet* Vol 336 No 8712 pp 430-431; *R v Adomoko* [1991] 2 MLR 277.

14. *R v Prentice and Sullman* (1993) NLJ 850.

The basis on which the two doctors were convicted was that they had both created an obvious and serious risk of causing serious harm, which they had nevertheless had gone on to take, or alternatively that they had taken the risk without having given any thought to the matter (following the definition of recklessness in *R v Caldwell*). The judge in giving both doctors a nine month prison sentence suspended for two years did add however, 'It seems to me that you could have been helped much more than you were helped'.

Both doctors appealed against their conviction, and on appeal both convictions were quashed on the grounds that the trial judge had erred in failing to instruct the jury that excuses and mitigating circumstances could be taken into account when determining gross negligence. The Lord Chief Justice, Lord Taylor, held that in future, liability of medical practitioners for involuntary manslaughter was to be judged according to the test laid down by Lord Atkin in *Andrews v DPP*[15]. Thus the ingredients of involuntary manslaughter would in future consist of a breach of the doctor's duty which caused death, and gross negligence which the jury considered sufficient to justify a criminal conviction. A finding of gross negligence could be made on proof of evidence of one of the following states of mind:

* indifference to an obvious risk of injury to health; or

* actual foresight of risk coupled with a determination nevertheless to run that risk; or

* appreciation of the risk coupled with an intention to avoid it, but also coupled with a high degree of negligence in the attempt at avoidance; or

* inattention or failure to consider a serious risk which went beyond 'mere inadvertence' in respect of an obvious and important matter which the defendant's duty demanded he should have addressed.

It is important to note that the eventual acquittal of Doctors Prentice and Sullman had more to do with a disagreement among lawyers as to the application of a notoriously contentious test of criminal liability, than with the moral or legal culpability of the defendants themselves. Indeed it is arguable that if the correct test had been applied from the outset, both doctors would still have been convicted of manslaughter. After all it might well have been that the jury would have felt, on the facts, that the doctors had indeed failed to 'consider a serious risk in respect of an obvious and important matter which their duty demanded they should have addressed'.

Both doctors were in general medicine and not haematology; both doctors commenced work at the hospital only four weeks before the accident. The doc-

---

15. *Andrews v DPP* [1937] AC 576.

tor who actually gave the fatal injection was a pre-registration houseman who had been misled by a member of the ward staff who had told him that the patient was attending for his 'normal' lumbar puncture. The other houseman who supervised him did not know the nature of the drug to be injected. Neither had been trained in the use of cytotoxic drugs and the consultant in charge of the patient was unaware that these two doctors were administering the treatment which was not in accordance with the recommendations of the General Medical Council and the hospital's handbook. Furthermore, it would appear that the trained member of the nursing staff left the doctors to be assisted by two trainee nurses. The true cause of the tragedy thus appears to lie with a variety of staff, with the hospital, the health authority and even possibly the government for the inadequate funding of the hospital.

As result of the Court of Appeal's decision in this case it is possible to conclude that gross negligence manslaughter has survived the decision in *R v Caldwell* and will continue to be applicable in circumstances where death occurs as a result of a breach of duty owed by one person to another.

More importantly perhaps, as a result of the decision in *Sullman and Prentice*, there is now a new test as to what constitutes gross negligence manslaughter. This new test requires the jury to consider whether the risk taken by the defendant in the course of his duty was one which they (the jury) consider justifies a criminal conviction. Juries may thus become more influential in deciding which acts actually amount to criminal acts in future. Health professionals should be aware however, that the attitude of the general public towards those who carelessly cause death, is not a sympathetic one.

The Court of Appeal in *R v Scarlett*[16] said that the law of manslaughter was in urgent need of reform and it hoped that serious consideration will now be given to implementing proposals for a more modern and rational approach to the law of manslaughter. The Law Commission is to accelerate its review of the law of involuntary manslaughter and has recently produced a consultation paper on this topic.

Other criminal offences

Criminal assault involves the use or threatened use of unlawful force; the unlawfulness in the majority of cases stems from the lack of consent of the victim. Where the victim has apparently consented to the assault, even though that consent was obtained by deceit or fraud, this consent is sufficient to exonerate the defendant.

A person may only consent to surgery for valid purposes recognised by the

---

16. *R v Scarlett* (1993) *The Times* 7 May.

criminal law; the consent is only valid so long as the operation is for therapeutic purposes. This will cover medically prescribed treatment even though the treatment may involve a risk of harm to the patient because the possible therapeutic benefits of the operation are said to outweigh the possible risks. Thus even a sex change operation performed for therapeutic purposes is lawful and will not give rise to a criminal prosecution for assault of the doctor who carried it out. However if a person were to have a limb amputated in order for instance to avoid military service or so that he could claim a disability allowance, his consent would be invalid and the surgeon would be liable for criminal assault occasioning actual bodily harm as the operation would have no therapeutic purpose.

The area of cosmetic surgery is problematic since it can be argued that it has at least in some cases no therapeutic value; however the argument generally advanced is that cosmetic surgery has psychological benefits to the patients, and is thus therapeutic. If, however, a doctor carried out cosmetic surgery so that the patient could avoid detection for a crime, then this would not be for a therapeutic purpose and the consent would be invalid.

In several criminal cases the defence of necessity has been used to defend doctors against criminal charges. Thus in *Bourne*[17] an obstetric surgeon was charged with unlawfully using an instrument with intent to procure a miscarriage, contrary to the Offences Against the Person Act 1861 s 58 having performed an abortion on a 14 year old girl who had been the victim of rape. The defendant doctor was acquitted on the grounds that he was not acting unlawfully if he had acted in good faith to save the girl's life.

> ... the unborn child in the womb must not be destroyed unless the destruction of the child is for the purpose of preserving the yet more precious life of the mother (*per* McNaghten J).

A similar approach was adopted in *Gillick v West Norfolk & Wisbech AHA*[18], where the House of Lords stated that a doctor who prescribed contraceptive treatment for a girl under the age of 16 years would not be guilty of aiding, abetting, counselling or procuring the offence of unlawful sexual intercourse committed by her with a man, provided he honestly believed the action to be necessary for the physical, emotional and mental health of the child. Lord Scarman stated:

> The bona fide exercise by a doctor of his clinical judgment must be a complete negation of the guilty mind which is an essential ingredient of the criminal offence of aiding and abetting the commission of unlawful sexual intercourse.

---

17. *R v Bourne* [1938] 3 All ER 615.

18. *Gillick v West Norfolk & Wisbech AHA* [1986] AC 112.

In a more recent House of Lords decision on necessity In *Re F (Mental Patient: Sterilisation)*[19], it was held to be lawful to carry out a sterilisation operation on a mental patient who lacked the capacity to consent as there was a grave risk that she would become pregnant, which would have had disastrous psychiatric consequences for her. Lord Goff stated that where action was taken to preserve the life, health or well being of another who is unable to consent to it, such action would not be criminal provided that:

- there must be a necessity to act when it is not practicable to communicate with the assisted person; and

- circumstances dictate, acting in the best interests of the assisted person.

Where a defendant inflicts an injury upon a victim which requires medical treatment, who is to be held criminally liable if that treatment is so improper or negligent that the victim dies? In some cases it has been claimed by the defendant that the true cause of death was not the original criminal act of assault, but rather the medical treatment received by the patient once in hospital.

In *Jordan*[20] D stabbed V who was taken to hospital where the wound was stitched; eight days later V died. At the time of death the wound had healed and D had died as a result of a terramycin injection to prevent infection (administered after V had shown an intolerance to terramycin) and the intravenous introduction of large quantities of liquid which caused V's lungs to become waterlogged. This was an example of a case where the medical treatment was so palpably poor, that it could be said to have broken the chain of causation between the defendant's criminal act and the death of the patient (although this did not necessarily impose criminal liability on those who had treated him).

Not all bad medical treatment will break the chain of causation in this way however; in *Cheshire*[21] the patient's original wounds necessitated medical treatment, but the immediate cause of death was a respiratory infection which developed post operatively following a tracheotomy and caused severe respiratory obstruction. This occurred because V's windpipe had become obstructed due to narrowing, a rare but not unknown complication of the procedure. While there was evidence that the medical team had failed to diagnose and treat this problem the court held that the operating and substantial cause of death remained the original wounds caused by the acts of the defendant.

Where the victim of a criminal attack is treated for wounds or injuries by a doctor or other medical staff attempting to repair the harm done, it will only be in the most extraordinary and unusual case that such treatment can be said to

---

19. In *Re F (Mental Patient: Sterilisation)* [1990] 2 AC 1.
20. *R v Jordan* (1956) 40 Cr App R 152.
21. *R v Cheshire* [1991] 1 WLR 844.

be so independent of the acts of the defendant that it could be regarded as the cause of the victim's death to the exclusion of the defendant's acts.

One ground on which the decisions in *Jordan* and *Cheshire* might be reconciled is that the law requires the accused to take as normal the quality of medical treatment which is given in an emergency, when medical staff are under pressure, even though in other circumstances it might appear that such treatment was quite inappropriate. The test to be applied therefore, would be 'did the medical treatment provided reach a reasonable standard, given the conditions of urgency under which it was given?'.

An alternative way of reconciling the decisions is to suggest that in *Jordan* the victim's wound was virtually healed, and therefore no longer capable of acting as a cause of death, whereas in *Cheshire* this was not the case. This seems a less satisfactory approach for if the ground for distinguishing cases is that in one the wound is capable of causing death and in the other it is not, this rests the decision on the moment in time when the wrong treatment was given. For example, if A who is seriously injured after an attack is given the wrong treatment immediately he is admitted to hospital, whereas B who has been similarly injured is given the wrong treatment two weeks later, it may follow that the first death is a homicide by the defendant and the second is not. A's assailant is denied the chance to show that the wound, although of a very serious type, would not have killed A if proper treatment had been given.

It would appear that it is only in rare cases where treatment is given by operation or prescription of drugs that medical negligence will supervene to become an independent cause of death. Examples might be where a poison is accidentally administered to the patient, or a drug is administered in an excessive quantity which leads to the patient's death, or where a drug is administered to which the patient has already displayed an intolerance.

In recent years problems have also arisen with respect to patients who have suffered serious injuries at the hands of an assailant and whose life is being temporarily sustained by a life support machine. If the machine is finally switched off by the doctors caring for him, are they criminally responsible for the patient's death. In the cases of *Malcherek* and *Steel*[22] M had stabbed his wife with a kitchen knife causing a deep abdominal wound, and S had attacked a girl causing her grave head injuries. Both victims were put on life support machines during the normal course of treatment. In each case the victims received normal and conventional medical treatment and in each case the life support machines were switched off after a number of tests indicated that brain death had occurred. Both M and S were convicted of murder and appealed on the grounds that by switching off the machines, the doctors rather than the assailants, had caused the victims' death.

---

22. *R v Malcherek; R v Steel* [1981] 1 WLR 690.

However, as Lord Lane CJ stated:

There is no evidence ... that at the time of conventional death, after the life support machinery was disconnected, the original wound or injury was other than a continuing, operating and indeed substantial cause of the death of the victim ... it is somewhat bizarre to suggest ... that where a doctor tries his conscientious best to save the life of a patient brought to hospital in extremis, skillfully using sophisticated methods, drugs and machinery to do so, but fails in his attempt and therefore discontinues treatment, he can be said to have caused the death of the patient.

Thus, the court decided that it was not the act of the doctor in discontinuing life support that was responsible for the patients' death, but rather the original criminal offences which caused the injuries in the first place.

CASE STUDY ONE

Asif, a child of 24 months, was seriously handicapped at birth following a road traffic accident to his mother during her pregnancy. Asif, who is unable to see or hear and is in constant pain, is continuously sedated and fed artificially via a feeding tube implanted in his stomach. His parents believe that Asif should be permitted to die and ask his doctor to withdraw nutrition and hydration from him.

Advise Asif's doctor.

CASE STUDY TWO

Betty gave birth to a child, Clare, who suffered from Down's syndrome. Betty told the consultant pediatrician, Dr Don, that she did not wish her baby 'to survive' and this was recorded in the medical notes. Thereafter, Dr Don prescribed 5mg dihydrocodeine at the discretion of the nurse in charge of the baby 'as required' and 'nursing care' only. Clare developed pneumonia.

What action should the nurse in charge of this baby take?

5 Litigation by Parents and Children for Pre-birth Events

The common law

For many years there was judicial doubt as to whether a child once born has a right of action against a tortfeasor who caused him injury prior to his birth. Indeed in the Canadian case of *Montreal Tramways v Leveille*[1] Lamont J said that 'the great weight of judicial opinion in the common law courts, denies the right of a child when born to maintain an action for pre-natal injuries'.

In this country prior to 1976 it was assumed, in line with Lamont J's comment that there was no legal liability for negligently injuring a foetus; however the terrible effects of the drug Thalidomide on unborn children, and the subsequent litigation was based on the assumption that such a cause of action existed (*Distillers Co (Biochemicals) Ltd v Thompson*[2] – this case was finally settled out of court so that the matter was never judicially decided).

In a later Canadian case *Watt v Rama*[3], a pregnant woman who had been injured by the negligent driving of the defendant gave birth to a child who, at birth, was found to suffer brain damage and epilepsy and was paralysed from the neck down. Here the court had to decide whether, at the time of the accident, the negligent driver owed the foetus a duty of care; following the basic negligence principles established in *Donoghue v Stevenson*[4] (see p 2), the court held that it was reasonably foreseeable that at the time of the collision the defendant's actions might cause injury to a pregnant woman in the car with which he was in collision, and that therefore the possibility of his causing damage to the child she was carrying was also reasonably foreseeable. This gave rise to a duty of care owed by the defendant to the foetus which only became effective in law if and when that child was born alive. The reason that birth was identified as the moment when the legal relationship arose, was because this was the point at which the child suffered injuries as a living person.

In the same year, in *Duval v Seguin*[5] Fraser J in the High Court of Ontario held, applying *Donoghue v Stevenson*, that an unborn child was:

---

1. *Montreal Tramways v Leveille* [1943] 4 DLR 339.
2. *Distillers Co (Biochemicals) Ltd v Thompson* [1970] 1 WLR 715.
3. *Watt v Rama* [1972] VR 353.
4. *Donaghue v Stevenson* [1932] AC 562.
5. *Duval v Seguin* (1972) 26 DLR (3d) 418.

... within the foreseeable risk incurred by the negligent motorist. When the unborn child becomes a living person and suffers (injuries) as a result of pre natal injuries caused by the negligent motorist, the cause of action is completed.

The judges in these cases carefully avoided the question of whether the foetus itself had a legal status, arguing instead that since it is essential in negligence to show that the plaintiff has suffered damage, and the damage is not suffered until the birth of the child, the tort against the child is completed at the moment of live birth.

There were several English cases however, where it was assumed that the foetus did have a legal status although the matter was never raised for discussion in the litigation; thus in *Whitehouse v Jordan*[6] where a child was born with injuries which were caused during the process of birth ie prior to the child being born alive, it was assumed that an action could be brought on behalf of the child for the injury suffered.

However, in 1992 in two separate cases (*Burton v Islington HA*[7] and *De Martell v Merton & Sutton HA*[8]) the English courts held that a common law duty to the foetus exists. These cases, concerned two children who had been born with severe abnormalities. In the case of *Burton* these arose after her mother had been subjected to a dilation and curettage procedure when five weeks pregnant; she alleged that failure to perform a pregnancy test prior to the operation amounted to negligence on the part of hospital staff. In the case of *De Martell* it was alleged that negligence by medical staff at the time of delivery and birth had caused the plaintiff's injuries. Both children were born in 1967.

At trial Phillips J, in finding for the plaintiffs, said:

To my mind it is but natural justice that a child if born alive and viable should be allowed to maintain an action in the courts for injuries wrongfully committed upon its person while in the womb of its mother.

The Court of Appeal upheld the decision of Phillips J and held in both cases that a plaintiff injured as a foetus, had a common law right to bring a cause of action in negligence against a health authority even though the actual negligent act was performed on the mother.

In the cases discussed above, the tort that has caused injury to the foetus has been committed following conception. However, a child may also be harmed as a result of a tort which took place *prior* to his conception; there are no English cases which suggest that at common law a duty is owed to such a child.

---

6.   *Whitehouse v Jordan* [1981] 1 WLR 24.

7.   *Burton v Islington HA* [1991] 1 All ER 825.

8.   *De Martell v Merton & Sutton HA* [1991] 2 Med LR 209.

However in Australia in the case of *X and Y v Pal*[9] there are dicta which imply that no distinction should be drawn between children injured by pre conception wrongs and those injured by torts committed during pregnancy. In this case the plaintiff, who had already given birth to one grossly deformed child who had died shortly after birth, gave birth to a second, similarly deformed, because she was suffering from syphilis. She claimed, on behalf of her second child, that she should have been screened for syphilis after the birth of the first child and before she became pregnant with the second; it was this failure to screen which caused the severe mental subnormalities and disfigurement suffered by the second child who was a plaintiff in this case. Clarke JA, who decided the case in favour of the plaintiffs, held that in principle there is no distinction between pre-conception occurrences and those *in utero* which cause harm to the unborn child:

> In principle ... it should be accepted that a person may be subjected to a duty of care to a child who was neither born nor conceived at the time of his careless acts or omissions such that he may be found liable in damages to that child. Whether or not that duty will arise depends upon whether there is a relevant relationship between the careless person and the class of persons of whom the child is one ...

Two unreported English cases based on the concept of paternal pre-conceptual irradiation (PPI) were brought against British Nuclear Fuels Ltd in 1993; these plaintiffs' claims broke new grounds, being the first in this country in which compensation was sought for pre-conception damage, allegedly caused by radiation to an adult's genes, passed on to future offspring. The first plaintiff was Elizabeth Reay whose baby daughter died of leukemia in 1962 and whose case was considered under the common law rules applied in *Merton* and *De Martell*; the second was Vivienne Hope born in 1965 who developed non-Hodgkins Lymphoma in 1988 and has been left infertile and partially disabled. They claimed that their fathers had been exposed to high doses of radiation which contaminated their sperm and created a predisposition in their children to develop cancer. The defendants, BNFL, denied responsibility and in October 1993 in the High Court, French J ruled 'decisively' in favour of the defendants, on the grounds that in the absence of supporting evidence, on the balance of probabilities BNFL were not to blame. The plaintiffs were refused legal aid to appeal against this decision. The most obvious difficulty experienced by such claimants, is proof of a causal nexus between eg the radiation exposure, and the injury actually suffered.

An even more remote possibility is where the tort of the careless defendant causes injury to the victim's grandchild. While, in principle, this should be subject to exactly those consideration discussed in p 72 above, in practice the courts

---

9.   *X and Y v Pal* (1991) 23 NSWLR 26.

are not anxious to extend liability so far. In *Enright v Ely Lilly & Co*[10] the question arose as to whether the drug diethylstilbestrol (DES) should extend to a 'third generation' plaintiff who was the granddaughter of the woman who had been prescribed this drug. It was alleged in this case that the plaintiff's injuries were caused by her premature birth, which in turn was caused by damage to her mother's reproductive system, caused by her mother's ingestion of DES while pregnant.

The New York Court of Appeal rejected the plaintiff's claim in this case on the grounds of policy factors, since to find in favour of the plaintiff would extend the traditional tort concepts 'beyond manageable bounds' ie the number of potential plaintiffs would be so great as to be unfair to the defendants and to run the risk of 'opening the floodgates' to a mass of litigation.

Where a child is born dead as a result of a tort committed while the child was unborn it seems that in English law there is no cause of action; there can be no actionable breach of duty to those born dead: before they are born they are not persons and after they are born they have no legal rights.

Statute

Following the Thalidomide tragedy and the subsequent recommendations of the Law Commission Report (Cmnd 5709) in 1974 the Congenital Disabilities (Civil Liability) Act 1976 was enacted and applies to all births occurring after 22 July 1976. Children born prior to this date remain subject to the common law as described above.

The Act requires the child plaintiff, suing by his next friend, to establish that his injury was caused by an 'occurrence' as defined in s 1(2) of the Act; an occurrence is one which:

• affected either parent in his or her ability to have a normal healthy child;

• affected the mother during her pregnancy; or

• affected the mother or the child in the course of its birth.

Section 1(3) makes the defendant liable to the child if he was also liable in tort to the parent (or would have been, if sued in due time). It is no answer that the parent would have suffered no actionable injury as a result of the tortious act, provided there was a breach of duty which, if accompanied by injury to the parent, would otherwise have given rise to liability.

For liability to be incurred, the Act requires that the child should be born alive, either disabled, or with disabilities; s 4(1) states that the child must suffer:

---

10. *Enright v Ely Lilly & Co* (1991) 570 NE 2d 198 (NYCA).

... any deformity, disease or abnormality, including predisposition (whether or not susceptible of immediate prognosis) to physical or mental defect in the future.

This limits the operation of the Act to damage which is assessable in pecuniary terms to avoid the situation in *Williams v State of New York*[11], where the
plaintiff sued for 'wrongful life' she claimed to have suffered; in this case the
defendants had, by their negligence, allowed the plaintiff's conception to occur.
However, the disability complained of (being born out of wedlock to a mentally
defective mother) would not fall within the terms of the Act since there is no
assessable pecuniary value which can be determined.

A similar judgment was reached in the English case, *McKay v Essex Area
Health Authority*[12] where the courts held that there was no duty to cause the
death of a foetus infected by rubella. A claim by the plaintiff was struck out by
the court as disclosing no reasonable cause of action in English law.

Section 1(5) of the Act covers the position of the medical practitioner as a
result of whose act an unborn child is injured. Under the Act a doctor is not
liable for the child's injuries providing that he took reasonable care, having due
regard to the then received professional opinion, applicable to the particular
class of case.

It would appear that this is a statutory equivalent to the common law rule in
the *Bolam* test (see Chapter 1); what is less clear is whether the section refers to
failure to warn as well as to specific treatment.

Under the Act a child's right of action is derived from the parent's, ie it is
based on the breach of a legal duty to the parent; being derivative it follows that
defences may be mounted based on the conduct of the parent eg: under s 1(4)
any voluntary assumption of risk by the parent (subject to the provisions of the
Unfair Contract Terms Act 1977) will amount to the defence of *volenti*; s 1(7) also
provides a defence in relation to the parent's contributory negligence which can
be raised as a defence in the normal way.

The typical pre-conception event to which the Act would apply includes
physical injury to woman's pelvis prior to conception, radiation injury to either
parent, a negligent blood transfusion causing illness to either parent (eg venere-
al disease or HIV), the negligent supply (by donor) or handling (by medical
staff) of male sperm for artificial insemination purposes, negligent X-ray treatment injuring either parent or defective contraceptive substances or devices
causing injury to the child. Thus liability was admitted and compensation over
£330,000 was awarded to a girl born handicapped due to the negligent transfusion of blood to her mother seven years before her birth (*Roberts v Johnstone*[13]).

---

11. *Williams v State of N York* (1966) 18 NY 2d 481.

12. *McKay v Essex Area Health Authority* [1982] 1 QB 1166.

13. *Roberts v Johnstone* (1986) *The Times* 26 July.

The basic rule that a child cannot sue his mother for injuries suffered *en ventre sa mere* does not apply where the injury arises as a result of his mother's careless driving (s 2). This exception permits the child to benefit from the mother' motor insurance.

The Act provides that the tort against the parent, on which the child's claim is based, is to be considered without reference to the normal time limitations imposed by the Limitation Act 1980 (ie normally, actions for personal injuries must be brought within three years of the infliction of the relevant injury). While it is well known that plaintiffs who suffer mental handicap at birth as a result of negligent medical treatment can delay litigation for the period of their life plus three years, it is less well understood that victims of pre-conception or pre-birth negligence can delay the issue of a writ *indefinitely*.

Wrongful life

A 'wrongful life' claim is one in which the plaintiff asserts that as a result of negligent conduct by the defendant he or she was born, and that if there had not been negligence on the defendant's part, the birth would not have occurred. Typical examples include negligent genetic counselling, negligent selection of an embryo for implantation or negligent testing of a foetus for genetic defects. Most of the cases to date involve very serious and harmful conditions which affect the infant although the term 'wrongful life' was first used in a case where a healthy infant claimed that he had been injured by being born to less than optimal parents, ie that his father had allowed him to be born illegitimate. In all 'wrongful life' cases the plaintiff is the child or his agent (not the parents of the child).

(a)   The common law

Initially, in the common law jurisdictions, such actions failed; thus in an American case, *Gleitman v Cosgrove*[14], a child who was born deaf mute and almost blind because his mother had contracted German Measles during her pregnancy, failed in his action against the doctor who had advised the child's mother that German Measles afforded no risk to her unborn child. However many of the American states have now recognised the right of an infant to sue for wrongful life; the California case *Curlender v Bio-Science Laboratories*[15] for instance, involved a child born suffering from Tay-Sachs disease. The parents of the child were awarded damages against the doctor who negligently told them that they were not carriers of the disease.

---

14. *Gleitman v Cosgrove* (1967) 296 NYS (2d) 689.
15. *Curlender v Bio-Science Laboratories* (1980) 165 Cal Rptr 47.

It is important to remember that the claim in a wrongful life case is not that the defendant has caused the disabilities of the child, but rather that by failing to inform parents adequately, the doctor is responsible for the birth of a disabled child who would otherwise not have been born, and therefore would not have experienced the suffering caused by his disabilities.

The English courts considered a 'wrongful life' claim in *McKay v Essex Area Health Authority*[16]; in this case the plaintiff was infected as a foetus with rubella and was born partially sighted and deaf; she claimed that the doctor who treated her mother was negligent in that he failed to advise her mother to have the foetus aborted and that she therefore suffered damage by her entry into a life in which she suffers from debilitating injuries. Ackner LJ with whom the other judges agreed held that:

> I cannot accept for the moment that the common law duty of care to a person, can involve, without specific legislation to achieve this end, the legal obligation to that person, whether or not in utero to terminate his existence. Such a proposition runs wholly contrary to the concept of the sanctity of human life.

He then went on to discuss the damage which the plaintiff claimed she had suffered as a result of the doctor's negligence:

> What then are the injuries which the doctor's negligence has caused? The answer must be that there are none in the accepted sense ... She cannot say that, but for his negligence, she would have been born without the disabilities. What the doctor is blamed for is causing her, or permitting her, to be born at all ... But how can a court begin to evaluate non existence, 'the undiscovered country from whose bourn no traveller returns?' No comparison is possible and therefore no damage can be established which a court could recognise.

By contrast with the US jurisdictions the English courts have not been sympathetic to 'wrongful life' claims, holding that the gift of life is of such value that it would be against public policy to allow a plaintiff to recover damages on the basis that it would have been better had he or she never been born.

(b)   Statute

The Congenital Disabilities Act 1976 was based on the recommendations of the Law Commission in its Report in 1974 (No 60 Report on Injuries to Unborn Children):

> We do not think that in the strict sense of the term, an action for 'wrongful life' should lie ... Such a cause of action would place an almost intolerable burden on medical advisers in their socially and morally exacting role. The danger that doctors would be under subconscious pressures to advise abortions in doubtful cases through fear of an action for damages is, we think, a real one.

---

16. *McKay v Essex AHA* [1982] QB 1166.

Thus, in *McKay's* case (see p 77 above) the Court of Appeal interpreted s 1(2)(b) of the Act as not applying to 'wrongful life' claims. Lord Justice Ackner held that the subsection is so worded as to import the assumption that, but for the occurrence giving rise to the disabled birth, the child would have been born normal and healthy, not that it would not have been born at all.

Wrongful conception

This section considers the question whether parents may bring an action against a doctor whose negligent advice or treatment has led to the birth of a healthy (but unwanted) child. This situation usually occurs following a failed sterilisation operation, or a failed abortion.

Where the sterilisation or abortion procedure has been carried out privately, rather than under the auspices of the National Health Service, then there is a contract between the patient and his consultant, and between the patient and the hospital where he is treated. If it appears that a consultant is in breach of his contract, for example, then a patient who suffered damage as a result of that breach would have a cause of action against him in contract.

However, it is rare for a doctor to be so incautious to guarantee sterility following a sterilisation operation. Thus in *Eyre v Measday*[17], a woman who had undergone an operation to sterilise her subsequently became pregnant. She sued her doctor claiming that he had guaranteed the success of the operation. The Court of Appeal dismissed her claim, and Slade LJ held that:

> On the facts of the present case I do not think that any intelligent bystander (let alone another medical man) on hearing the discussion which took place between the defendant and the other two parties, could reasonably have drawn the inference that the defendant was intending to give any warranty of this nature (that the operation would be completely successful) ... But in my opinion, in the absence of any express warranty, the court should be slow to imply against any medical man an unqualified warranty as to the results of any intended operation.

Nowadays it is common for the consent form for sterilisation operations to explain fully the risk of failure and possible future fertility, and thus claims of this sort are very unlikely to occur in the future.

Where a patient is treated under the provisions of the National Health Service there is no contract between the patient and his doctor; thus the only cause of action open to such a patient who had given birth to an unwanted child as a result of failed sterilisation or abortion operation would be to sue in the tort of negligence. In such a case the normal legal requirements as to duty of care,

---

17. *Eyre v Measday* [1986] 1 All ER 488.

breach and causation would apply (see Chapter 1 for a full treatment of these issues).

However, it is worth mentioning here the case of *Thake v Maurice*[18] where both the sterilised patient and his wife sued their doctor claiming that he had been negligent in not informing them of the chance that the effects of the vasectomy operation might be naturally reversed; the court held that the doctor had been negligent and awarded compensation to the parents. In his judgment Peter Pain J said:

> In approaching this problem I firmly put sentiment on one side. A healthy baby is so lovely
> a creature that I can well understand the reaction of one who asks how its birth could possi-
> bly give rise to an action for damages. But every baby has a belly to be filled and a body to
> be clothed. The law relating to damages is concerned with reparation in money terms and
> this is what is needed for the maintenance of the baby.

The position is now clear, therefore, that in English law at least, unwanted children are a potential ground for litigation and compensation; general damages for pain and distress during pregnancy as well as the cost of the baby's upbringing are recoverable. However, the facts of a recent case, *Danns v Dept of Health*[19] would seem to be pushing the bounds of such actions too far; in this case the plaintiffs became parents eight years after the husband's vasectomy, and are currently suing the Department of Health for failing to publicise the possibility of natural reversion and consequent pregnancy. The research on which their claim is based indicates a risk of recanalisation of 0.04 per cent, and although the plaintiffs have been granted legal aid it is unlikely in our opinion that they will be successful if the case proceeds to trial.

Wrongful birth

This term applies to a claim brought by the parents of a child who was born disabled as a result of negligence which occurred before it was born; this might occur for instance where a doctor failed to inform potential parents of the increased possibility that a mother would give birth to a child suffering from birth defects, thereby precluding an informed decision as to whether they should have a child.

An example of this type of situation is provided by the facts of the American case *Harbeson v Parke-Davis*[20] where the plaintiff mother had been given medication (Dilantin) to control her epileptic seizures, but had not been warned that any children which might subsequently be born to her would possibly suffer

---

18. *Thake v Maurice* [1986] QB 644.

19. *Danns v Dept of Health* (1992) 305 BMJ 912

20. *Harbeson v Parke-Davis* (1983) 656 P 2d 483.

from 'foetal hydantoin syndrome'; the plaintiffs claimed that if they had been warned of this possibility they would not have gone on to have further children. The parents were awarded damages for the birth of two affected children which included figures to represent the medical, educational and other expenses attributable to the disabled condition of the children. The court did not, however, allow the parents damages which would have represented the costs of raising a normal healthy child but only those damages causally connected with the disabilities from which the children suffered. It is interesting to note that although the plaintiffs claim for wrongful *life* was unsuccessful in *McKay v Essex AHA*, the plaintiffs claim for wrongful *birth* in the same case, was successful.

CASE STUDY ONE

Amanda, who was in the first trimester of her pregnancy, contracted German Measles. She visited her doctor and requested that he treat her with gamma globulin to reverse any damage that might have been caused to her unborn child. The doctor reassured Amanda that such treatment was unnecessary. Amanda subsequently gave birth to Ben who was born partially blind and deaf. Amanda now wishes to sue her doctor, on behalf of Ben on the grounds that he should have advised her to have an abortion, which advice she would undoubtedly have accepted.

Advise Amanda.

CASE STUDY TWO

Charles and Diana were concerned about their daughter Enid, who appeared to have hearing difficulties. Acting on the advice of their pediatrician they were referred to a specialist clinic for evaluation of a possible hearing defect. Enid was examined and tested by Frank, a specialist in the diagnosis and treatment of hearing defects., who advised her parents that her hearing was 'within normal limits'. In fact, Enid was totally deaf as a result of a hereditary condition. Enid's parents did not learn the true nature of Enid's disability until some months later, by which time a second child, Grace, had been conceived. In an action brought on behalf of G, who is also totally deaf, they now seek damages from Frank for the extraordinary expenses of specialised teaching and training, and the provision of hearing equipment.

Charles and Diana also seek compensation on their own behalf for the emotional distress caused by caring for a totally deaf child.

Advise Charles and Diana.

6 Liability for Drug Induced Injuries

Background

Historically the patient's physician was also his apothecary who both pre-scribed and dispensed his drugs; indeed the concept of the pharmaceutical company is of relatively recent origin, the oldest companies being little more than 100 years old. However, drug companies have only taken over a part of the traditional role of the physician which was to devise, prepare and prescribe remedies. The role of the doctor in treating his patients remains the same, and he continues to take responsibility for his use of a particular remedy in treating a particular patient.

Over the past 50 years, however, the development by pharmaceutical companies of new products ranging from those designed to combat serious conditions (eg high blood pressure, heart disease) to those designed for convenience (eg anti nausea drugs, the contraceptive pill) and those designed for cosmetic purposes (eg silicone breast implants) have brought huge profits to the pharmaceutical companies which developed them and benefits to many patients for whom they were prescribed. However it has become clear that these developments have been accompanied by a substantial increase in litigation by patients aggrieved, or even fatally damaged, by the side effects of the products themselves.

In this country public awareness of the possibly disastrous side effects of pharmaceutical products began in the early 1960s with the publicity surrounding the effects of Thalidomide; this drug was developed by a West German firm, Chemie Grunenthal, and manufactured and sold in this country under licence by a British company, Distillers. Thalidomide was a sedative considered to be safe for pregnant and nursing mothers, but which appeared to have caused gross foetal abnormalities in the children of many of those for whom it was prescribed.

Since the 1960s there has been a worryingly large number of pharmaceuticals which appear to have given rise to adverse side effects: these include Opren (an anti-rheumatic drug: 1981); Debendox (an anti nausea drug for use during pregnancy: 1983); Eraldin (hormone pregnancy tests: 1971), Myodil (an opaque dye used in the diagnosis of back injuries: 1990), the whole range of Benzodiazepines, produced by different manufacturers (prescribed for the treatment of anxiety and sleep disorders: 1988) and Copper 7 (an intra-uterine contraceptive device: 1991). There has also been a claim by a group of haemophiliacs who were infected by the AIDS virus as a result of being transfused with contaminated blood; this latter claim was settled by the government making payments on an ex gratia basis.

To date, there is apparently no reported English case in which damages have been awarded for drug induced injuries[1], although some English litigants have been successful in the US courts (eg English women sued the manufacturers of the Dalkon Shield contraceptive device in the US and have received compensation from a settlement fund set up in the US when the manufacturers of the product went into liquidation).

As the law now stands, liability in respect of pharmaceutical products can, theoretically at least, arise in a variety of ways: there may be liability for breach of contract, for breach of the duty of care owed under the tort of negligence (see Chapter 1 above), under the provisions of the Consumer Protection Act 1987 or, in a limited number of cases, under the Vaccine Damage Payments Act 1979. These alternative and sometimes overlapping possibilities will be considered in the following sections of this chapter.

Liability in contract

The manufacturer of medical products owes a number of duties relating to the goods which he manufactures and sells. These duties arise from the contract of sale and are therefore only owed to the immediate buyer. Implied terms become a part of the contract by the Sale of Goods Act 1979 as amended by the Sale of Goods Act 1994, which requires the goods sold to be fit for their purpose (ie they must be reasonably fit for the purpose for which they are sold: s 14 (3)). They must also be of satisfactory quality (ie they must be in a reasonable state to be sold at the price charged: s 14(2)).

There have been remarkably few reported cases of manufacturing defects in drugs (a notable example was the supply of ampoules of hydrocortisone which had been accidentally filled with vecuroniam[2]) and manufacturers might point to the efficacy of their quality control processes by way of explanation. A cynic might argue however that such cases tend to be settled out of court without recourse to litigation.

The difficulty in distinguishing manufacturing defects from design defects was illustrated by the recent litigation brought by haemophiliacs who became HIV positive following their transfusion with contaminated blood products imported from America (Factor VIII). The plaintiffs alleged that the contamination could have been prevented by heat treatment. However, at the time, the

---

1. The litigants in the Myodil claim were reported (*The Times*, 1 August 1995) as having settled their claim against Glaxo, for a figure of approximately £16,000 per claimant.
2. See 'Patients get drug after mix up' *The Guardian*, 29 June 1985.

manufacturing standard did not require heat treatment because the danger of such contamination was unknown, thus what appeared to be a manufacturing defect, was in fact a design issue.

When drugs are sold directly to a patient they must meet the standards required by the Sale of Goods Act in exactly the same way as any other goods purchased. However, it would be very unusual for the producer of a pharmaceutical product to have entered into a contractual relationship with the patient and in the case of prescription only drugs the manufacturer probably only enters into such a relationship with the wholesaler, who in turn has a contractual relationship with the retail pharmacist or rural dispenser.

Thus it is that the pharmacist is usually the only person to have a contractual relationship with the patient, and then only if the drug is purchased over the counter (eg a brand name cough remedy) or dispensed privately where the patient pays the full cost of the drug directly to the pharmacist (ie not under the provisions of the National Health Service). Under these circumstances the provisions of the Sale of Goods Act 1979 as amended by the Sale of Goods Act 1994 referred to briefly above become a part of the contract between the pharmacist and the patient. If the drugs purchased or prescribed in these circumstances are unfit or not of satisfactory quality, then the seller will be strictly liable for any damage which results to the patient. Thus as will be seen from the remainder of this chapter, a patient who has actually purchased for himself the drug which damaged him will be in a more favourable position than other patients. If he can prove to the satisfaction of the courts, that the drug was unfit or of unsatisfactory quality then the pharmacist will be strictly liable in the law of contract for any damage which results. It will be no defence for the retailer of the drug, or the pharmacist who dispensed it, to argue that he was not at fault, or that given the state of medical knowledge at the time it would have been unreasonable to expect him to foresee the injuries which in fact occurred.

These contractual remedies are not of any substantial assistance to the majority of patients who claim to have been injured by the drugs they have taken. Severe side effects do not tend to be caused by patent remedies bought over the counter, and patients for whom drugs have been prescribed within the provisions of the National Health Service cannot benefit from the requirement for fitness for purpose and for satisfactory quality in the Sale of Goods Act since they have not entered into a contractual relationship either with the manufacturer or the pharmacist. Even though such patients will often have paid for their drugs this payment is defined as a statutory charge, and the pharmacist will have dispensed the drug as part of his contract with the local Family Health Services Authority, not with the patient.

Liability in the tort of negligence

The majority of patients who suffer injury as a result of drugs have been prescribed them within the provisions of the National Health Service. Under these circumstances the only cause of action available to such a patient under the common law is in the tort of negligence (see Chapter 1 which describes in some detail the basic principles relating to the law of negligence).

The publicity given to the effects of Thalidomide on unborn children, was the catalyst for an attempted reform of personal injury law in Britain, as it become plain that the negligence system was totally inadequate as a means for compensating the victims of this tragedy[3]. However, in order to be successful in such an action a patient will need to demonstrate that there was a breach of the duty of care owed to her by the manufacturer or the pharmacist or the prescribing doctor which caused the injuries of which she complains.

In an action against the importer or manufacturer the plaintiff will need to prove that the defendant pharmaceutical company owed her a duty of care and was in breach of it, through the negligent design or manufacture of the drug.

The manufacturer will have fulfilled this duty if he can show that the product is of a reasonable design (ie that all reasonable research has been carried out through clinical trials and all relevant scientific knowledge taken account of in the design of the product) and that the manufacturing process is such as to meet the appropriate standard of quality, safety and efficacy. In this sense the position of the manufacturer of drugs differs in no way from the manufacturer of any other product who produces drugs:

> ... in such a form as to show that he intends them to reach the ultimate consumer in the form in which they left him, with no reasonable possibility of intermediate examination, and with the knowledge *that the absence of care in the preparation or putting up of the products will result in injury to the plaintiff's life* or property, will owe a duty to the consumer to take that reasonable care (*Donoghue v Stevenson*[4]) (emphasis added).

Similarly a drug manufacturer may be found liable for breach of duty if it can be proved that the necessary warnings and/or instructions as to use, eg dosage or contra indications, were not been made available to the patient and/or the doctor.

As a matter of common law it is well settled that a manufacturer of a product has a duty to warn consumers of dangers inherent in the use of its product of

---

3. See eg The Law Commission's Report 'Liability for Defective Products' (1977) Law Com No 82, Cmnd 6831 and the Royal Commission on Civil Liability and Compensation for Personal Injury (1978) Cmnd 7054 (the Pearson Report).
4. *Donoghue v Stevenson* [1932] AC 562.

which it knows or has reason to know. Whether a particular warning is adequate will depend on what is reasonable in the circumstances. But the fact that a drug is ordinarily safe and effective and the danger may be rare, or only involve a small percentage of users, does not necessarily relieve the manufacturer of the duty to warn *per* Robins JA in *Buchan v Ortho Pharmaceuticals (Canada) Ltd*[5]. The warning should be such as to permit a competent person to protect himself and others against any dangerous properties of the drug.

Moreover it seems clear that the manufacturer cannot rely on the prescribing doctor (under the 'learned intermediary' rule) to warn patients of dangers and contra-indications, unless all necessary steps have been taken by the company to warn the doctor.

> A drug company cannot rely upon doctors to read all the scientific literature outlining the specific dangers involved in the many drugs that they have to administer each day. They are busy people, administering to the needs of the injured and the sick. They have little time for deep research into medical literature. They rely on the drug companies to supply them with the necessary data ... The doctors should have as full information as is reasonable in the circumstances ... (*per* Linden J in *Davidson v Connaught Laboratories*[6]).

In addition the manufacturer will also be under a duty to give adequate directions on the proper use of the product. This is particularly important in respect of drugs such as antibiotics and contraceptives where frequency and timing are crucial to the drug's effectiveness.

Where a plaintiff brings an action against the prescribing physician the plaintiff must prove not only that her doctor owed her a duty of care, but also that he was in breach of this duty, in that he negligently prescribed the drug which caused her injuries. Such a breach of duty may have consisted of prescribing the drug in the wrong quantity (see eg *Dwyer v Roderick*[7]) or when she had already demonstrated an intolerance to it. If the action is brought against the dispensing pharmacist, the plaintiff must also show that he owed her a duty of care and was in breach of it, eg that he negligently dispensed the wrong drug or indicated the wrong dosage (see eg *Prendergast v Sam & Dee* [8]) where the liability was shared between the doctor whose handwriting on the prescription was so poor that the pharmacist could not read it, and the pharmacist because he dispensed a drug that was clearly inappropriate for the patient in question).

As indicated above, there is no recorded case in this country of a plaintiff successfully suing a manufacturer for drug-induced injuries. Clearly there are financial and emotional difficulties involved in any form of litigation, which deter potential plaintiffs from claiming damages. If a plaintiff does embark on

---

5.   *Buchan v Ortho Pharmaceuticals (Canada) Ltd* (1986) 54 OR (2d) at 92.

6.   *Davidson v Connaught Laboratories* (1980) 14 CCLT 251 (Ont HCJ0) at 276.

7.   *Dwyer v Roderick* (1983) 127 SJ 806.

8.   *Prendergast v Sam & Dee* (1989) *The Times* 14 March.

litigation however, she will encounter considerable practical difficulties in proving that the defendant has acted in breach of the duty of care owed to her: the standard of care which the courts will require of the defendant will be that generally prevailing at the time that the relevant drug was produced.

Thus, for example while it is now well known that some types of drug can damage a foetus at sensitive stages of development, this was not widely known at the time when Thalidomide was first marketed. Thus it could not be argued by the plaintiffs that the manufacturers and importers of Thalidomide were in breach of their duty of care to the consumers of the drug, since they could not at the time reasonably be expected to foresee the damage. The effect of this legal rule is that a drug manufacturer will not be said to have acted negligently (in breach of his duty of care to the patient) if the state of scientific knowledge at the time that the drug was put on the market was not such as to enable him reasonably to foresee the injury which in fact occurred.

A further difficulty for plaintiffs is that even if they are able to show that a defendant was in breach of his duty of care, it is still very difficult to prove as a matter of fact, and to the standard required by the civil law (on the balance of probabilities), that this breach has actually caused the injuries of which they complain. In many cases the plaintiff was already ill when she took the drug, and it thus very difficult to disentangle the effects of the drug from the natural progress of the patient's illness to prove that the defendant's breach of duty was the true cause of the plaintiff's injury.

Yet another difficulty to be faced by potential litigants is that not every adverse drug reaction indicates a fault in the product. Idiosyncratic reactions and or hypersensitivity can occur in susceptible individuals without there necessarily being any defect in the product in question. (Indeed if all products causing such reactions were to be found defective, then there would be few medical products on the market, since the majority of drugs cause adverse reactions in some people. Even the humble aspirin which has been available for almost 100 years causes adverse reactions in a surprisingly high proportion of the population.)

The Consumer Protection Act 1987

The EC directive on product liability enacted in Part I of the Consumer Protection Act 1987 altered the duty owed by a manufacturer of products put into circulation within the European Community. The directive was intended to harmonise the law on product liability in the member states, and to make manufacturers 'strictly liable' for injuries caused by their products, and the English statute was intended to enact the provisions of that directive.

The concept of strict liability for products is a simple one: where a plaintiff can show that the product in question was defective under the 1987 Act (s 3(1)(1)), and that the product caused his injury, he will be entitled to compensation.

This liability is imposed on all 'producers' of goods; the term 'producers' here includes not only the original manufacturer, but also importers under licence, 'own-brand' suppliers and even, under some circumstances, an ordinary distributor of the product, even though none of these may have been responsible for the actual manufacture of the product. The 'producer' may also liable, under the statute for defective component parts manufactured by another company, if they are incorporated into the finished product.

Under the Act the 'producer' of the product is only liable for injuries caused by it, if the product can be shown to have been 'defective'. A product is defined as 'defective' if it is not as safe as people are generally entitled to expect (s 3(1)).

This definition is elaborated in s 3(2) which requires that in determining whether a product is 'defective', consideration should be given to 'the manner in which, and the purposes for which, the product has been marketed, its get-up, the use of any mark in relation to the product and any instructions for, or warnings with respect to, doing or refraining from doing anything with or in relation to the product'.

This test is clearly based on 'fault' and would appear to be very little different from the common law test for negligence; and raises queries about whether in truth the Act does have the effect of imposing strict liability on 'producers' as was intended in the EC directive.

Insofar as drugs are concerned, it is well known that almost every drug carries an associated risk, but this does not mean that every drug is therefore 'defective' under the Act. A drug will only be 'defective' where it can be shown that the risks associated with its use are so grave that they outweigh the potential benefits of treatment.

The date at which the 'defective' nature of the product is to be determined is the date when the product left the control of the producer; thus if safety standards become higher between leaving the control of the producer and the use of the product by a patient, then the 'producer' will not be liable under the Act.

The Act also makes provision for a number of defences, the effect of which is to introduce significant fault elements into what was said to be a strict liability regime. In particular, the controversial 'state of the art' or 'development risks' defence (s 4(1)(e)) allows a producer to escape liability if he can prove that the state of scientific and technical knowledge at the time that the product left the producer's control was not such, that 'a producer of products of the same description as the product in question might be expected to have discovered the defect' if it had existed in the product at the time that it was under the producer's control. As Atiyah has commented 'This latter defence is simply a plea of "non negligence" in the designing, development and testing of the product'[9]. The government was not required by the directive to include this defence in the Act as this was an option to be left to the discretion of member states; however of the first seven countries to implement the directive only Luxembourg did not avail itself of the option.

Currently there are no reported English cases which consider the application of the Act to pharmaceutical products, however the US case *Brown v Superior Court (Abbot Laboratories)*[10] is indicative of the line likely to be taken by the courts. In *Brown* the court held that:

- a drug manufacturer's liability for a defectively designed drug should not be measured by the standards of strict liability;

- because of the public interest in the development, availability and reasonable price of drugs, the appropriate test for determining responsibility is the test stated in comment K to the Restatement Second of Torts (ie that the producer of a properly manufactured prescription drug should only be held liable for injuries cased by the product if it was not accompanied by a warning of dangers of which the producer was aware or should have been aware).

It would appear that the Consumer Protection Act 1987 may well be interpreted in this country in the same way as American law has developed in *Brown*; if it does, this will bear out the undoubted truth of Lord Scarman's comment in the debate in the House of Lords when the 'state of the art' defence was being discussed.

If you introduce the state of the art defence you are really introducing negligence by the back door[11].

The only apparent advantage of s 4 to the consumer is that it would appear to reverse the burden of proof; under the common law a plaintiff is required to prove on the balance of probabilities that the defendant was in breach of his duty of care, while under the Act it would appear that the burden now falls on the defendant to show that the risk of which the plaintiff complains was not known to him or capable of being known (see *Feldman v Lederle Laboratories*[12]).

The DHSS circulars (HN(88)3 and HN(FP)(88)5), which deal with the implications of the Consumer Protection Act for the National Health Service, advise hospitals that health authorities may be liable as the supplier of a defective product to a patient, unless the producer or the authority's supplier can be identified. It would appear to be of some importance therefore, that hospital records

---

9.   P Crane (ed) (1983) *Atiyah's Accidents Compensation and The Law*, London: Butterworths.

10. *Brown v Superior Court (Abbot Laboratories)* (1988) 751 P 2d 470.

11. 414 HL deb col 1427.

12. *Feldman v Lederle Laboratories* (1984) 479 2d 374 (NJ Sup Ct).

clearly show from whom and when a product was obtained and to whom and when it was supplied, including any serial or batch number, the date of its issue to wards and clinics and it should be noted in writing that all due warnings and instructions about its use were passed on.

Second the DHSS also states that a health authority may be liable as a 'keeper' for damage from defective products that it uses, if the product's supplier or the producer show that the equipment has not been adequately maintained, calibrated or used in accordance with instructions. This is an added reason for keeping full records as to use and maintenance.

Third a health authority may also be liable as a 'producer' itself, eg of medicines, appliances, dressings, blood products, products from hospital pharmacies etc.

The Vaccine Damage Payments Act 1979

The Royal Commission on Civil Liability and Compensation for Personal Injury recommended that where vaccine damage can be proved to have followed from medical procedures advocated by the government then a child should have the right to bring an action in tort on the basis of strict liability against the government. It would appear to be the case that a small proportion of children suffer severe brain damage and other injury, as a direct result of the national vaccination programme against such illnesses as tetanus, diphtheria, whooping cough, measles and poliomyelitis. In such cases it has always been very difficult to establish causation, because small children not infrequently develop convulsions and other symptoms of brain damage in the first two years of life, and only some of these attacks follow routine vaccination. Manufacturers of the vaccines in question argue that the symptoms are caused in fact by congenital damage or concurrent infection rather than the vaccine itself.

Vaccination is said by economists to be a classic case of the 'free rider' problem. The benefit to each individual child of the vaccination programme may not be very great, since the majority of other children will be vaccinated and thus the risks of an unvaccinated individual child developing these illnesses is small. Yet if all parents withdrew their children from the vaccination programme the diseases in question would spread more rapidly at a greater risk to all and a greater cost to the state.

The obvious remedy for a parent who believed that his child had suffered serious injury as a result of the national vaccination programme would be to sue in the tort of negligence, alleging either that the vaccine was defective in some way, or that the doctor who had administered the vaccine had done so negligently. The advantage of such an action would be that in the event that the litigation was successful, the child would receive full compensation for any handicap caused by the vaccine. However, as will be seen from the discussion of cases below, it is by no means clear that the vaccine has actually been the medical *cause* of the damage of which plaintiffs complain, and an action against the administering doctor is likely to fail through the application of the *Bolam* test (ie the majority of the medical profession still believe the vaccine to be safe).

A plaintiff must establish both a cause of action and causation in order for a claim to be successful. The cause of action is usually alleged to be negligence in administering the vaccine despite contra-indications (although there have been some trespass claims as well). However general causation issues must be tackled successfully by the plaintiff too (ie can the vaccine cause this type of damage) as well as specific causation issues (in any particular case, did the vaccine in fact cause the damage of which the plaintiff complained.)

There has been litigation in the UK based on injuries alleged to have been caused specifically by the pertussis vaccine (which protects against whooping cough) against manufacturers, the Department of Health, doctors and health authorities. At least 200 claims have been initiated either at common law in negligence or under the Vaccine Damage Payments Act 1979.

The Vaccine Damage Payments Act was introduced by the Government in 1979 in response to mounting public pressure; it provides for a lump sum payment of £30,000 (claims since 1988) to any person who can be shown to have suffered 80 per cent disablement as a result of one of the specified vaccinations administered after July 1948.

Claims must be made in the first instance to the Department of Health and, where the department official is not satisfied that the claim is made out, the claimant may ask for the decision to be reviewed by a specially constituted tribunal. The claimant must have been vaccinated when under the age of 18 years (except in the case of rubella and poliomyelitis) and must prove causation on the balance of probabilities to the satisfaction of the official or the tribunal.

By s 1 the plaintiff must show he or she was 'severely disabled' ie 80 per cent disability) as a result of vaccination of the plaintiff (or of the plaintiff's mother prior to birth). The diseases covered by the Act are:

- diphtheria;

- tetanus;

- whooping cough;

- poliomyelitis;

- measles;

- rubella;

- tuberculosis;

- smallpox; and

- any other disease specified by the Secretary of State.

The requirement on the plaintiff to prove a minimum of 80 per cent disability has meant that many potential plaintiffs have been prevented from claiming compensation under the Act.

By s 2 vaccination must have been carried out within the UK or Isle of Man after 5 July 1948 (or, in the case of smallpox, 1 August 1971); the plaintiff must have been under the age of 18 at the time of vaccination and over the age of two at the time that the claim was made, or the plaintiff must have died.

Claims must be made within the period of six years beginning on the latest of the date of vaccination, or the date on which P became two years old, or 9 May 1978. This is a requirement which has meant that many plaintiffs whose parents were unaware of the possibility of recovering compensation under the Act are out of time and thus unable to claim.

A decision on any claim is reached initially by the Secretary of State (in reality officers from the Department for Health) who must be satisfied on the balance of probabilities that the damage was caused by the vaccine. An appeal for review of this decision lies to the local Vaccine Damage Tribunal which must decide:

- the extent of the child's disablement;

- whether the child's disablement is 'severe'; and

- the issue of causation.

Suing the Department of Health under the Act has been a process fraught with difficulty. Thus in *DHSS v Kinnear*[13] it was held that no cause of action can arise out of a policy decision made in good faith by the DHSS, pursuant to the provisions of the National Health Service Act 1946, s 26 to make arrangements concerning the immunisation of people against infectious diseases. A cause of action could lie however in respect of operational decisions taken by the DHSS (in this case regarding advice as to the circumstances in which immunisation is carried out).

Proving causation, even within the no-negligence system of strict liability under the Act, has also been a considerable problem. In *R v Vaccine Damage Tribunal ex p Loveday*[14] the plaintiff applied to Secretary of State for compensation under the Act; when this application was refused the plaintiff appealed to the Vaccine Damage Payments Tribunal which rejected the appeal on causation grounds. A subsequent appeal to the High Court quashed the Tribunal decision

---

13. *DHSS v Kinnear* (1984) 134 NLJ 886.

14. *R v Vaccine Damage Tribunal ex p Loveday* (1985) The Lancet 1137.

on the grounds that proper reasons had not been given, and that the possibility of aggravation of pre-existing brain damage had not been considered. A re-rehearing was ordered, at which an award was again refused. The High Court then quashed the decision of the second Tribunal on evidential and procedural grounds, but still refused to make an order directing it to find a causative link between vaccination and damage. The plaintiff's mother then appealed to the Court of Appeal which concurred with the refusal to issue an order, on the grounds that there was insufficient evidence to conclude that the child's condition resulted inevitably from the vaccination (but did not rule out the possibility of directing a Tribunal as to causation in future cases).

Following this decision in 1985, all pertussis claims either under the Act or in negligence were assigned to Stuart-Smith J (as he then was). He then reheard *DHSS v Kinnear* as a test case in 1986 when it became apparent that the plaintiff would fail on the issue of negligence as the plaintiff's mother had lied about the facts, and the case collapsed after 29 days, legal aid having been withdrawn.

A second test case was then selected which was *Loveday v Renton*[15]. In this case the plaintiff sued her GP for negligence in administering vaccine in disregard of one or more contra-indications, thus causing brain damage. The case lasted 63 hearing days and the judgment runs to 230 pages with 50 pages of appendices. The court held on the causation issue that:

- P had failed to show on a balance of probabilities that pertussis vaccine could cause permanent damage in young children;

- it was possible that it did;

- the contrary could not be proved.

Stuart-Smith J added that even if the preliminary issue of causation had been resolved in favour of P it was unlikely that negligence could have been proved.

At this stage it appeared that the problems of proving that the pertussis vaccine had caused injuries to any plaintiffs (whether suing in negligence or under the Act) were insuperable. However, in 1990 in *R v Legal Aid Area No 8*[16] a case of seven conjoined applications against the refusal of a legal aid committee to assist the plaintiff's litigation under the Vaccine Damage Payments Act, Simon Brown J ruled that an earlier decision to refuse legal aid had been arrived at incorrectly in relation to a pertussis claim. Then in 1992 the Irish Supreme Court[17] accepted that pertussis vaccine *could* cause brain damage on the basis of new medical evidence not available at the time of *Loveday v Renton*. At this point it appeared that the Legal Aid Board had probably reviewed its policy in rela-

---

15. *Loveday v Renton* (1988) *The Times* 31 March.

16. *R v Legal Aid Area No 8* (1990) *The Times* 13 March.

17. [1994] Med LR 81.

tion to whooping cough claims and that this could give rise to as many as 400 new claims for compensation either in negligence or under the Act.

However it would now appear that such a view was premature. In May 1992 (*R v Legal Aid Board ex p S*[18]) Brooke J heard an application for judicial review against the Legal Aid Board which had refused legal aid to an infant plaintiff. The original action was based on a claim founded in negligence (rather than under the Vaccine Damage Payments Act) claiming that the plaintiff's GP had administered the vaccine despite the fact that she was suffering from a respiratory infection. The following day the child developed febrile convulsions which led to permanent brain damage. In his judgment Brooke J referred to the earlier judgment of Stuart-Smith LJ in which he quoted from the manufacturer's advice regarding contra-indications to the whooping cough vaccine:

> It is advisable to postpone vaccination if the child is suffering from any acute febrile illness, particularly respiratory, until fully recovered. (Minor infections without fever or systemic upset are not regarded as contra-indications.)

On the basis that the plaintiff's illness prior to vaccination was only minor, the court refused the application for judicial review.

The writers are forced to the conclusion therefore, that the Act deserves the criticisms that have been directed at it by legal academics[19]. The almost insuperable difficulties facing litigants in proving a causative link between vaccination and injury means that the Act does not provide an adequate statutory compensation mechanism.

---

18. *R v Legal Aid Board ex p S* (1992.)LEXIS 14 May

19. See eg Brazier M (1992) *Medicine, Patients and the Law*, Penguin Books p 189.

CASE STUDY ONE

Jane buys a box of Sunshine Oil capsules from her local supermarket Sainsways. The box has a picture of a yellow flower on the front and on the back, in small writing, the instructions for use say 'Take one tablet twice a day'. There is no leaflet in the box.

The capsules have been purchased by Sainsways from a retailer, Severn Health Products in the UK, which in turn has imported the capsules from a manufacturing company, La Vie en Rose, in France. The manufacturing company imported the oil with which the capsules are filled from several local Turkish sources.

Jane, who is anxious to be fit, takes four tablets daily. After several weeks she becomes very ill, and is diagnosed as suffering from irreversible liver damage caused by the contents of the capsules.

Advise Jane.

CASE STUDY TWO

Ann, a childminder, takes Ben, a baby that she cares for from time to time, to the clinic for his second triple vaccination. The clinic nurse asks Ann if Ben displayed any signs of illness after the first vaccination. Ann replies that she assumes not as otherwise Ben's mother would not have asked her to bring the baby along to the clinic.

The doctor vaccinates the baby who, 24 hours later, suffers a series of convulsions which lead to permanent brain damage.

Advise Ben's mother.

7   Organ Transplantation and Tissue Donation

The living donor

Common law

By 1992 the number of patients in England awaiting kidney transplants alone had risen to just under 5,000 and it is clear that in this country at least, the demand for transplanted and donated organs of all types, far exceeds the supply. Earlier, in 1989, there had been a public outcry over the transplant of kidneys from impoverished Turkish nationals to rich 'queue jumpers' at the Wellington Humana Hospital in London. The Turkish donors had been recruited and paid to donate their kidneys to genetically and ethnically unrelated recipients, and in some cases seemed to be unaware of the fact that they now only had one kidney.

The first question to be considered is whether, at common law, an individual may lawfully consent to the removal of non-regenerative tissue from his body for the purposes of transplantation to another. Under medieval common law a person committed the crime of mayhem if he so injured another as to make him less able to fight to defend himself and his family. Thus, to amputate a limb, even with the patient's consent, was unlawful since it robbed the king of the services of a fighting man.

While the modern law has moved on from this position, the rights of an individual to donate non-regenerative organs from his body are not entirely clear for donor operations do not fulfil all the normal requirements which make modern surgical treatment lawful: thus, although they are carried out with the donor's consent, the operation has no therapeutic value to the donor and does carry an element of risk beyond the immediate dangers of anaesthesia and surgery It would appear that the modern common law test as to the lawfulness of these procedures is not whether the donor remains fit enough to defend himself, but rather the degree of bodily harm that the donor is likely to suffer.

The decision in *AG Ref No 6 of 1980*[1] seems to indicate that provided the donor consents to the transplant and risk benefit ratio is not manifestly to his disadvantage such operations are lawful:

> Ordinarily then if the victim consents (to injury) the assailant is not guilty ... the question is, at what point does the public interest require the court to hold otherwise? ... The answer to

---

1. *AG Ref No 6 of 1980* [1981] QB 715.

this question ... is that it is not in the public interest that people should try to cause or should cause each other bodily harm for no good reason ... Nothing which we have said is intended to cast doubt on the accepted legality of ... *reasonable surgical interference* (which) ... *can be justified as ... needed in the public interest* (*per* Lord Lane emphasis added)).

No donor could, at common law, consent to a transplant the result of which would be his own death, as this would not be in the public interest; one life would be saved, but only at the expense of another. Thus a donor could not donate his heart, or the whole of his liver, but probably could donate a kidney or a part of his pancreas. Recent developments in medical technology mean that in the near future it could become common for a donor to donate segments of his liver or lung tissue and this would appear to be lawful at common law.

A further difficulty is that transplant operations are non therapeutic for the donor; this issue has been considered by the courts and found to be lawful provided the necessary consent has been given.

In a US case *Bonner v Moran*[2], a court held a surgeon liable in trespass when a 15 year old boy consented to a skin graft being taken from his body to benefit that of his badly burned cousin, but only on the basis that he was not old enough to consent to the operation and that his parents' consent should have been sought. The court assumed that with lawful consent such an operation would itself have been lawful.

In conclusion it is probably true to say that providing a transplant is carried out with the donor's valid consent, it will be lawful at common law. However, in determining whether that consent is validly given the courts will consider:

- whether the cost–benefit ratio is too heavily weighted against the donor; and

- the nature of the non regenerative organ to be donated; and,

- the extent of physical harm to the donor at the time of the operation and in his future life.

If the court finds that the donor, however willing he may be to donate the relevant organ, would suffer undue pain or shortening of his life, then it is likely that such a procedure would be considered not to be in the public interest.

Minors at common law

Where the potential donor is a minor the question has to be asked whether s/he can consent to organ donation. If the principle in *Gillick v W Norfolk and Wisbech AHA*[3] is applied then the answer would be that such consent is valid where it can be shown that the minor in question is competent to understand the pro-

2.   *Bonner v Moran* (1941) 126 F 2d 121 (US CA DC).

3.   *Gillick v West Norfolk and Wisbech AHA* [1985] 3 All ER 402.

posed procedure, its effect and its future implications. However if the later decisions in *Re W*[4] and *Re R*[5] are correct then it could be argued that there are certain operations to which at common law, a minor cannot give his consent, and that the operation by which an organ transplant takes effect is one such procedure, since it could be argued not to be in the donor's best interests.

Statutory limitations on organ transplants

Following the extensive media coverage which followed the kidney transplants involving Turkish nationals, hurried legislation was enacted in this country to prohibit commercial dealings in human organs, and to restrict the transplanting of organs between persons not genetically related; the statutory regulation is now to be found in the Human Organs Transplant Act 1989[6].

Under s 1 of the Act, all *commercial* dealings in transplant organs is prohibited. An offence under the section is committed if, in Great Britain, a defendant either makes or receives payment having supplied (or having offered to supply) an organ which it is intended to transplant into another person anywhere in the world. An offence is also committed where a defendant is found to have sought a person willing to supply an organ for payment or initiates or negotiates any such arrangement or participates in the management or control of any business whose activities consist of the negotiation of such arrangements.

An organ is defined by s 7(2) of the Act as 'any part of the body consisting of a structured arrangement of tissues which, if wholly removed, cannot be replaced by the body'. This is thought to cover parts of the body not capable of regeneration, but would not include, for instance, blood products, bone marrow, semen, or skin. It does not cover human gametes and embryos which are covered by the Human Fertilisation and Embryology Act.

However a problem arises where only part of a non regenerative organ, is to be donated (eg the lobe of a liver). Here it is unclear whether such a procedure is covered by s 7(2) of the Act. Does the word 'part' in s 7(2) refer to the whole of the liver, in which case the Act does not apply to the transplant of the lobe, or does it refer to a part of the 'part', in which case the Act must apply.

An offence is also committed under the Act if D causes to be published or distributed in Great Britain an advertisement inviting people to supply (or offer to supply) organs, in return for payment (s 1(2)) where payment is interpreted

---

4.   *Re W* [1992] 4 All ER 627.

5.   *Re R* [1991] 4 All ER 177.

6.   Human Organ Transplants (Unrelated Persons) Regulations 1989, SI 1989/2480.

to mean for money or money's worth. This section does not however cover payments made to donors to reimburse their necessary expenses, eg the storing of an organ, the patient's travelling expenses or his loss of earnings.

Under s 2 D also commits the offence if, in Great Britain, he removes for the purposes of transplant, or transplants an organ, unless the transplant is between persons who are genetically related as defined in s 2(2) of the Act. Genetic relationships are very widely defined here, so as to include, for instance, such distant relatives as uncles and aunts of the half blood but obviously do not include spouses or spouses' relatives. The section requires that 'the fact of the relationship has been established by such means as are specified by regulations made by the Secretary of State. The Human Organ Transplants (Establishment of Relationship) Regulations 1989 (SI 1989/2107) provide for testing by approved testers using tests, which include DNA profiling.

However, transplants may lawfully be carried out between unrelated individuals if the transplant is carried out under the provisions of the Unrelated Live Transplant Regulatory Authority (ULTRA) set up under the Human Organ Transplants (Unrelated Persons) Regulations. These regulations permit the Secretary of State to authorise transplants between genetically unrelated persons if ULTRA is satisfied that:

- the transplant is not being carried out for payment;

- the donor has been appropriately counselled; and

- both donor and recipient have been interviewed.

Under regulation 3(2)(b) ULTRA is required to ensure that the donor understands the nature of the medical procedure and associated risks, that he or she consents to the removal of the organ in question and that such consent was not obtained by coercion or the offer of an inducement. It would seem that the main aim of ULTRA is to ensure that the donation of organs between unrelated donors and recipients is done on an altruistic rather than on a commercial basis.

A database of information about transplants carried out in Great Britain is kept in accordance with regulations made by the Secretary of State, and it is an offence to fail, without reasonable excuse, to provide the necessary information.

One question which has not yet been addressed by the courts but may well need to be in the near future, concerns the potential liability of a donor who donates an organ which subsequently causes harm to the recipient, perhaps because it is infected or genetically damaged. The donor's liability in Tort would probably arise from his (negligent) failure to disclose any genetic or other problems of which he was aware, and which he could reasonably foresee would cause injury to the recipient of the organ.

An analogous situation has been considered by the US courts where a sexual partner is infected with the HIV virus or other sexually transmitted disease. Thus in *Kathleen K v Robert B*[7] a woman who sued her former boyfriend for infecting her with genital herpes was awarded damages on the basis that the defendant's constitutional right to privacy regarding his condition was overcome by the state's interest in the prevention and control of contagious disease. The English courts might well reach a similar decision in relation to the failure of an organ donor to disclose any illness from which he or she knew he or she suffered.

A similar action might be brought against the Health Authority or trust hospital responsible for carrying out the transplant, if the recipient of the transplanted organ could prove that an employee was negligent in discovering the relevant information from the donor or in carrying out the appropriate tests. Thus in *Ravenis v Detroit Hospital*[8] a hospital was found to have negligently selected cornea donors and thus be liable in damages to the recipients. Similarly, in this country in *Re HIV Haemophiliac Litigation*[9] the Court of Appeal held that the government *could* owe a duty of care to those haemophiliac plaintiffs, who had been infected with the HIV virus as a result of blood transfusions. Health Authorities and hospitals owe a duty of care to their patients and in fulfilling that duty are required to protect patients from the effects of infected blood products. (Whether in this particular case there had in fact been a breach of this duty was never determined since in December 1990 the government agreed a settlement with the plaintiffs and the matter was never litigated.)

The position regarding so-called 'domino' transplants (heart and lung transplants to cystic fibrosis sufferers, which leave the recipient's heart available for further transplant) remains unclear. The subsequent implant of the recipient's heart would almost certainly be to a non-related patient, and thus, at least in theory would be unlawful; such transplants have to date not been challenged however, and the legal situation is uncertain.

Transplants from minors

The Family Law Reform Act 1969, s 8(1) provides that a person over the age of 16 years can consent to medical treatment without reference to parent or guardian (see Chapter 2). Insofar as the position of a minor under the age of 16 years is concerned, it has been argued that the law is as stated in *Re W*[10] in which it was held that a court can override the wishes of a mentally competent

---

7. *Kathleen K v Robert B* (1984) 198 Cal Rptr 273.

8. *Ravenis v Detroit Hospital* (1975) 234 NW 2d 411.

9. *Re HIV Haemophiliac Litigation* (1990) 962 NLJR 1349.

10. *Re W* [1992] 4 All ER 627.

minor, if it would appear to be in the minor's best interests to do so. It is unlikely that this principle would be applied by the courts to what would be described as the non-therapeutic treatment required for the purposes of a transplant. Indeed, in this case Lord Donaldson held that the Family Law Reform Act 1969, s 8(3) (which provides that: 'Nothing in this section shall be construed as making ineffective any consent which would have been effective if this section had not been enacted') applies only to treatment and diagnosis. He went on to say:

> Organ donations are quite different, and, as a matter of law, doctors would have to secure the consent of someone with the right to consent on behalf of a donor under the age of 18, or, if they relied on the consent of the minor himself, be satisfied that the minor was Gillick competent in the context of so serious a procedure which would not benefit a minor ... this would be a highly improbable conclusion.

Most commentators after *Re W* assume that although this would appear to confirm the common law rights of a minor under 16 years who understands the nature of the proposed treatment, and thus can give valid consent, this will not apply where the proposed treatment is not to the benefit of the child. It would seem that in English law no one under the age of 16 years can consent to the donation of non-regenerative tissue without the additional consent either of parents or of the courts, such consent only being given where it is to the child's benefit. It could be argued perhaps, as in the American case of *Strunk v Strunk*[11], that the loss of a sibling would be of greater harm to a child than the donation of a kidney which could keep that sibling alive.

There are undoubtedly powerful arguments why the law should prevent a minor, who may not understand the nature of organ donation and what it may entail, from making such decisions. Even where it would appear that the minor does show reasonable understanding of the procedure and its subsequent effects, it is argued that such donations should be limited to very close members of the donor's family (see LF Ross[12]).

Alternatively it may be that the principle that a minor cannot be subjected to any procedure which is not to his personal advantage is not necessarily an absolute one; the courts might decide for instance, that such a transplant was in the public interest.

---

11. *Strunk v Strunk* (1969) 445 SW 2d 45 (Ky CA).

12. L F Ross 'Moral Grounding for the Participation of Children as Organ Donors' (1993) 21 JL Med Ethics 251.

The Human Fertilisation and Embryology Act 1990

This Act specifically excludes from the ambit of the Human Organ Transplants Act 1989 those maternal and paternal relationships which derive from assisted reproduction, and which are recognised only by virtue of statute (see the Human Organ Transplants (Establishment of Relationship) Regulations[13].

The infertility treatments regulated by the Act cover only those which involve the use of donated genetic material (sperm, eggs or embryos), or those which involve the creation of an embryo outside the human body. The practice of surrogacy is not regulated by this Act but by the Surrogacy Arrangements Act 1985. The practice of artificial insemination which does not involve the use of donated sperm is not covered by the Act.

The Human Fertilisation and Embryology Act has the following functions:

* to license treatment, the storage of gametes and embryos and research on embryos (s 11);

* to monitor and inspect premises and activities carried out under license (s 9);

* to report annually to the Secretary of State on its activities (s 7); and

* to maintain a code of practice as guidance for the proper conduct of activities carried out under license (s 25).

The donor of genetic material and the recipient of that material must of course consent to the medical treatment involved s 13(6); in making this provision the Act merely reflects the common law position as to consent to treatment.

A more difficult issue is the extent to which the providers of gametes and embryos may exercise control over the future storage and use of their donated genetic material. Who will decide the fate of spare embryos after treatment is completed or abandoned. Schedule 3 of the Act requires that at the time that the genetic material is procured the donor must indicate in writing the use to which those gametes may be put to. The gametes or any resulting embryos must then only be used in accordance with the written intentions of the original donor. In particular, the maximum period of storage must be determined, as must the fate of the genetic material in the event of the death or incapacity of the donor.

The Consumer Protection Act 1987

This statute has already been discussed in the chapter dealing with liability for pharmaceutical products (see Chapter 6). The issue in this chapter is whether the so called 'strict liability provisions' of this statute (which is concerned with

---

13. Human Organ Transplants (Establishment of Relationship) Regulations 1989, SI 1989/2107.

liability for defective products) would apply also to the donation of organs which subsequently caused harm to the donee.

The main issue for consideration is whether an organ is a product for the purposes of this Act; in *Cunningham v McNeil Memorial Hospital*[14], the Illinois Supreme Court held that whole blood used for the purposes of transfusion is a product for the purposes of products liability law. In this country however it is likely that the provision by a health authority or trust hospital of blood or organs would be found to be the provision of a service rather than a of product. If this were to be the case then the Consumer Protection Act would not be relevant. If there were to be any statutory liability in respect of defective donated organs, it would be more likely to arise (if at all) under the provisions of the Supply of Goods and Services Act 1982.

Donation of tissue from corpses

At common law a corpse cannot be the subject of ownership; however the executor or next of kin has lawful possession of the body and is under an obligation to arrange for burial at the earliest opportunity. Moreover, at common law a man cannot by will, or otherwise, determine what will happen to his body after death. These limited common law rights regarding the disposal of remains were added to by the Corneal Grafting Act 1952, and then to a large extent replaced, by the Human Tissue Act 1961 (as amended), although the extent of overlap between the common law and statutory rules remains unclear.

The Act applies to dead donors ie where the brain stem of the patient has ceased to function even if the heart continues to beat (see *Bland v Airedale Health Authority*[15] for a discussion of the most recent judicial definition of death). Organ removal may be for therapeutic, educational or research purposes.

By s 1(1) of the Act it is provided that the removal of an organ from a dead body may occur lawfully if there has been a specific request to that effect by the deceased. However, the request must have been made by a competent person and it is not clear from the wording of the Act whether this requires the person concerned to be over the age of 16 years. The request may either be expressed in writing (it is unclear whether a signature is required) or may be made orally before two witnesses during the patient's 'last illness'.

By s 1(4) the transplant surgeon must establish that life is extinct, using established criteria and procedures for determining death.

Relatives have no *locus standi* to object to donation under s 1, unless there is evidence to show that the donor's instructions have been withdrawn before

---

14. *Cunningham v McNeil Memorial Hospital* (1970) 266 WE 2d 897.

15. *Bland v Airedale Health Authority* [1993] 1 All ER 821.

death; such a withdrawal of consent need not have been in writing but may be made orally. However, a coroner may veto any such authorisation if the death comes within his jurisdiction (s 1(5) and (9)).

In the absence of a specific request from the potential donor, s 1(2) provides for the authorisation of organ removal by the person 'lawfully in possession' of the body; this is thought to mean the person with physical possession of the body ie the hospital administrative officer (but not the next of kin, although they may have a right to possession at common law). This latter point is made clear by s 1(7) which empowers the hospital administrative officer to delegate his authority under s 1(2). If the person in possession of the body, has, after making such 'reasonable enquiry as may be practicable', no reason to believe that the deceased had any objection to organ donation, or that the surviving spouse, or any 'other surviving relative' of the deceased, objects to the body being so dealt with he may proceed to make transplant or other arrangements. An inquiry which incurred such delay as to make the organs therapeutically unusable, would probably be considered unreasonable.

It is becoming increasingly common for transplants from stillborn babies to take place; it is also becoming more common for a foetus to become an organ donor. A recent innovation is the removal of foetal brain tissue at 10-14 weeks gestation for transplant to elderly patients suffering from Parkinson's disease and other diseases of the brain. The Abortion Act 1967 (as amended 1990) permits an abortion on the grounds of foetal abnormality regardless of foetal age, and it is from such aborted foetuses that organs for donation may be acquired.

While the stillborn child is clearly covered by the relevant statute it is less clear what the legal position is in relation to foetal donation; it must be assumed that where the foetus is aborted it is considered to be 'dead' as a result of the process of abortion, and thus the foetus is covered by the Human Tissue Act rather than the Human Organ Transplant Act.

Curiously the Act does not provide any sanction for failure to comply with its requirements; however it has been suggested that the ancient crime of disobedience of a statute which is a common law crime may be relevant here (see *R v Lennox-Wright*[16] where this crime was said to be extant). In this case the defendant, who had failed his medical examinations abroad, gained admission to the ophthalmic department of an English hospital by false representations and forged documents. He then removed the eyes from a cadaver for their further use in another hospital, and was charged with 'doing an act in disobedience to a statute by removing parts of a dead body contrary to the Human Tissue Act 1961, s 1(4). Section 1(4) provides that 'no such removal shall be effected except by a fully qualified medical practitioner who must have satisfied himself by per-

---

16. *R v Lennox-Wright* [1973] Crim LR 529.

sonal examination of the body that life was extinct'.

This case can, however, be compared with *R v Horseferry Road Justices ex p Independent Broadcasting Authority*[17], where Lloyd LJ held that it requires clear language within a statute to create a crime.

---

17. *R v Horseferry Road Justices ex p Independent Broadcasting Authority* [1987] QB 54.

CASE STUDY ONE

Arthur and Ava have two sons, Tommy (28) and Jerry (25). Tommy is married with two children and is a graduate of the University of Bristol. He is employed as a history teacher in a local school. Unfortunately he suffers from chronic glomerulus nephritis and is now being kept alive by long term dialysis, a procedure which his doctors confirm cannot be continued for much longer.

Tommy's doctors also confirm that without a transplant he will at the least suffer very severe and progressive deterioration, and that there are no medically preferable alternatives to a kidney transplant.

Jerry has an IQ of approximately 35 and a mental age of 6 years; he is further handicapped by a speech defect which makes it difficult for him to communicate with others. Following tests it is discovered that he is the only member of his family who would be medically acceptable as a live donor of a kidney to his brother. A psychiatrist in the home where Jerry lives testifies that the death of Tommy would 'have an extremely traumatic effect upon Jerry'.

The dangers of the operation for Jerry are minimal; he is in good health and there is no evidence that he would suffer psychological harm.

What decision do you think the courts would reach if asked for a declaration that the transplant from Jerry to Tommy was lawful?

8 The Right to Refuse Treatment

A patient has the right to refuse any medical treatment, even that which may save or prolong life (*Barber v Supreme Court*[1]).

Introduction

The right of bodily integrity, to do what one wishes with one's own body, has long been established in law. This principle was followed for instance in the Californian case of *Bouvia v Supreme Court of California*[2] where a patient suffering from cerebral palsy was allowed to refuse artificial feeding and thereby end her life. The court made it clear in this case that a competent adult has the legal right to refuse treatment, even where the exercise of that right is likely to cause death.

It would appear that this principle applies equally where a patient has made a decision some time in the past, that a certain type of treatment will be unacceptable in the future. Thus, in the Canadian case of *Malette v Shulman*[3] an unconscious Jehovah's Witness was given a blood transfusion by a doctor, despite the fact that she carried a card which indicated her objection to such treatment. The defendant doctor argued that he need not observe this advance refusal of treatment since he could not be sure that the patient had not changed her mind since she made the decision, nor could he be sure that her refusal to be treated with blood products was fully informed at the time that it was made. The court rejected this reasoning however and held that the prohibition of treatment on the card should have been observed by the doctor in exactly the same way that he would have observed the stated wished of a conscious patient. Similarly in the English case of *Re T*[4] Staughton LJ commenting on the Canadian case stated: 'I doubt if the English courts would have awarded such a sum ($20,00); but the liability would still exist.'

It is estimated that approximately 9 per cent of the US public has executed some form of 'advance directive' stipulating how they wish medical treatment decisions to be handled in the event of their becoming incompetent[5]. In the UK,

---

1. *Barber v Supreme Court* (1983) 147 Cal App 3d 1006.
2. *Bouvia v Supreme Court of California* (1986) 275 Cal Rptr 297.
3. *Malette v Shulman* (1988) 63 OR (2d) 243 (Ont High Ct).
4. *Re T* [1992] 4 All ER 649.
5. Gelfand, 'Living Will Statutes: The First Decade' [1987] Wis LR 737.

the Voluntary Euthanasia Society has distributed 'living will' forms since the early 1970s, and their use have also been supported by Age Concern, which in conjunction with the Centre for Medical Law and Ethics, produced a working party report on 'The living will; consent to treatment at the end of life'[6]. The Terence Higgins Trust produced a living will form in 1992 which is designed to take effect when the declarant becomes 'unable to communicate and cannot take part in decisions about my medical care'[7] and in November 1992 the British Medical Association published a statement on advance directives which strongly supported them in principle as it sees them as giving 'significant benefits ... within the framework of continuing doctor-patient dialogue'. The BMA is not, however, in favour of the 'living will' being legally binding although it clearly accepts that doctors will normally comply with its contents. Where doctors have a conscientious objection to curtailing treatment in accordance with the patient's earlier stated wishes the BMA believes that they should have the right to transfer that patient's care to another practitioner[8].

The Law Commission has, however, recommended that legislation should be passed which would give statutory recognition to 'anticipated decisions' which would bind doctors[9]. It further recommends that a person should have the right to appoint a 'medical treatment attorney' to make treatment decisions on that person's behalf on incompetency. No provision exists for such powers of attorney in English law, for at common law any power of attorney lapses immediately the person who has granted the power becomes incompetent. The Enduring Powers of Attorney Act 1985, although extending powers beyond the onset of incompetence, only covers decisions regarding the grantor's (that is, the person granting the power of attorney) property, not his person; thus any nominated attorney would lack legal authority at the very point where the grantor intended it should come into effect.

Living wills

A statement refusing treatment in advance has become known as a 'living will' or 'advance directive'; it is usually a signed document giving advance instructions about an individual's future treatment. Typically it is used to declare that in the event that the individual suffers terminal and painful illness, or unconsciousness, or is reduced to a persistent vegetative state at some time in the

6. Lush, D, 'Advance Directives and Living Wills' (1993) Jnl RCPL 27:3, p 274.
7. Copies of the Living Will form are available from the Terence Higgins Trust, 52-54 Grays Inn Road, London WC1X 8JU, Tel: 0171-405 2381.
8. British Medical Association; Statement of Advance Directives. London, BMA November 1992.
9. See the Law Commission's Consultation Paper, No 129; Mentally Incapacitated Adults and Decision-Making: Medical Treatment and Research (1993).

future, sustaining or life-prolonging treatment will be withheld or withdrawn. It can also contain instructions about the appointment of a health care proxy who would have the right to be consulted by medical staff and have the authority to make decisions and represent the declarant's views in the event of mental incapacity. Conversely, the declarant could make a 'life prolonging declaration'[10] outlining the circumstances in which he wished to be kept alive for as long as reasonably possible.

The validity of the 'living will' document has not yet been tested in the English courts although the decision of the House of Lords in the recent case of *Bland v Airedale Health Authority*[11] indicates that it will almost certainly be enforceable at common law. In this case Lord Keith stated that:

> ... it is unlawful, so as to constitute both a tort and the crime of battery, to administer medical treatment to an adult ... without his consent ... such a person is completely at liberty to decline to undergo treatment, even if the result of his doing so will be that he will die. This extends to the situation where the person, in anticipation of ... entering into a condition such as PVS, gives clear instructions that in such event he is not to be given medical care, including artificial feeding, designed to keep him alive.

Lord Goff in the same case stated that:

> ... the same principle applies where the patient's refusal to give his consent has been expressed at an earlier date before he became unconscious, or otherwise incapable of communicating it; though in such cases special care may be necessary to ensure that the prior refusal of consent is still properly to be regarded as applicable in the circumstances which have occurred.

For an anticipatory refusal of medical treatment to be effective at common law it must meet four important criteria:

- the patient must be competent at the time of refusal: he must be conscious, free from the influence of drugs, and not be suffering from any mental illness;

- the patient's free will must not have been overborne by the influence of a third party;

- the patient must have been sufficiently informed of the nature and effect of the treatment which is being refused (or consented) to; the Court of Appeal in *Re T*[12] did not create a doctrine of 'informed refusal' but instead held that

---

10. See, eg the 'Life-prolonging procedures declaration' in the State of Indiana's Living Wills and Life Prolonging Procedures Act 1985.

11. *Airedale NHS Trust v Bland* [1993] 1 All ER 821; *Re T* (*Adult: Refusal of Medical Treatment*) [1992] 4 All ER 649.

12. *Ibid.*

a refusal may be valid provided the patient is aware of the 'nature and effect' of the treatment he is refusing;

- the refusal must cover the actual situation in which the treatment is needed.

The final criterion may allow the courts (and doctors) the ability to 'undermine the law's apparent commitment to a patient's right to self-determination'[13]. If a living will is not drafted in other than general terms it might be comparatively easy to argue that it was not intended to apply in the circumstances which subsequently arise. Indeed living wills are usually made when illness is but an abstract concept to the declarant and it is possible that the person's views may change over time.

There is evidence from the US that in the analogous situation of the Jehovah's Witness who refuses blood transfusion in advance of surgery the courts will be ready to infer that the advance refusal was not given with the specific circumstances in mind. Thus in *Werth v Taylor*[14] the plaintiff, having given birth to twins, underwent surgery for the curettage of the uterine lining to prevent further bleeding; two months earlier she had completed a 'refusal to blood transfusion' form. During the course of the operation the plaintiff's blood pressure dropped rapidly and in order to save her life a blood transfusion was performed. The judge held that her earlier refusal to be treated with blood products was not taken when her life was hanging in the balance nor when it appeared that death might be a possibility if a transfusion were not given. Thus the advance refusal was ineffective because, only 'the patient's fully informed contemporaneous decision ... is sufficient to override evidence of medical necessity'.

Furthermore, the terminology of many living wills, as evidence in the United States demonstrates, is often unclear thus giving rise to uncertainties as to their application. Thus, the 'living will' used in the state of Florida states that when a person is in a terminal condition 'life-prolonging procedures (may) be withheld or withdrawn when the application of such procedures would serve only to prolong artificially the process of dying'. Can it, for example, be inferred that the signatory of such a will categorically wishes to forgo such life saving procedures as cardiopulmonary resuscitation?

Indeed research evidence from the US suggests that, of those people who had made a living will, over one-third had not communicated this fact to their doctor, nor had they specifically discussed their cardiopulmonary resuscitation preferences[15].

---

13. Kennedy, I and Grubb, A (1994) *Medical Law*, London: Butterworths.

14. *Werth v Taylor* (1991) 475 NW 2d 426.

15. Walker, RM, Schonwetter, RS, Kramer, DR and Robinson, BE (1995) 'Living Wills and Resuscitation Preferences in an Elderly Population' Arch Intern Med Vol 155 January 23.

Furthermore, research in the UK indicates that 'patients who are acutely unwell may make decisions that are influenced by their condition at this point in time and it is important to recognise that these decisions may not be maintained'.

The Terence Higgins Trust living will form recommends that declarants discuss their intentions with a doctor and, where this is done, the form provides for the name and address of that doctor. It allows for a declarant to give instructions about both general and particular forms of medical treatment and to have his wishes temporarily disregarded while a named person(s) is given the opportunity to make contact with the declarant. A health care proxy may also be appointed and the will is required to be witnessed by a person over the age of 18 years, who is not a relative, potential beneficiary or appointed health care proxy or spouse or partner of the declarant.

Although the legal validity of such a will has never been tested in the English courts it is assumed on the basis of the House of Lords judgment in *Bland* that an advance directive would be legally binding; thus a doctor who acts in contravention of its provisions would be liable for battery both under the civil law of tort and under the criminal law. However, a doctor would have a defence available if he could argue that the will was not sufficiently clearly drafted to cover the medical situation prevailing, or that there was evidence that the declarant has since changed his mind.

The remaining problem, which the courts have not as yet been required to address, is whether the effectiveness of a living will could cease by mere passage of time. The longer the time period between the making of the living will and the onset of the relevant incapacity the greater may be the doubts as to whether the declarant's wishes have changed in the intervening period. The BMA recommended that they be revised every five years but there is no reason to believe that the English common law would make a presumption of automatic revocation after any given period of time.

The right of children to make living wills

There is no indication on the Terence Higgins Trust's living will form that the declarant should be over the age of 18. The Family Law Reform Act 1969[16] provides that a person aged 16 years and over may give a valid consent to medical treatment. Furthermore the House of Lords has made it clear[17] that a person who is under the age of 16 years who is of sufficient understanding and intelligence is also capable of giving valid consent in English law. The question arises as to whether a person under the age of 18 has a comparable right to refuse

---

16. Section 8(1).
17. *Gillick v West Norfolk and Wisbech Area Health Authority* [1986] AC 112.

treatment, particularly in circumstances where this will inevitably lead to death. In two important cases[18] the Court of Appeal held that a minor's right to refuse medical treatment was not synonymous with his right to consent to such treatment. While it accepted that a minor child below the age of 16 has the right to consent to treatment 'when the child achieves a sufficient understanding and intelligence to enable him or her to understand fully what is proposed'[19] and that such consent could not be challenged by the parents (or others with parental responsibility), the judges accepted that the refusal of consent by the competent child (under the age of 18 years) could be overridden by parents or the courts.

Thus a minor's capacity to make a valid living will stipulating the circumstances in which he wished to have life saving treatment withheld is doubtful. However, when Tony Bland went to support Liverpool in their match against Nottingham Forest at Hillsborough he was only 17 years of age. The court's judgment seems to accept, albeit implicitly, that a minor's declaration about future medical treatment in such circumstances would be legally recognised[20].

The Law Commission's proposals

The Law Commission makes the following important proposals:

- legislation should provide for the scope and effect of anticipatory decisions;

- if a patient is incapacitated (subject to the caveats discussed below) a clearly established anticipatory decision should be as effective as the contemporaneous decision of the patient would be in the circumstances to which it is applicable;

- there should be a rebuttable presumption that an anticipatory decision is clearly established if it is in writing, signed by the maker (with appropriate provision for signing at his direction), and witnessed by (one) person who is not the maker's medical treatment attorney;

- an anticipatory decision should be regarded as ineffective to the extent that it purports to refuse pain relief or 'basic care', including nursing care and spoon-feeding;

---

18. *Re R (a minor) (wardship: medical treatment)* [1991] 4 All ER 177; *Re W (a minor) (medical treatment)* [1992] 4 All ER 627.
19. *Per* Lord Scarman in *Gillick* (n 17) at 423.
20. See *Airedale NHS Trust v Bland* (n 11).

- an anticipatory decision may be revoked orally or in writing at any time when the maker has the capacity to do so. There should be no automatic revocation after a period of time;

- a treatment provider who acts in accordance with an apparently valid and continuing anticipatory decision should only be liable to any civil or criminal proceedings if he or she does so in bad faith or without reasonable care;

- it should be an offence to falsify or forge an advance directive; or to conceal, alter or destroy a directive without the authority of its maker. These offences should apply to a written revocation of an advance directive as they do to the directive itself.

Pregnancy

It is important to note that the Law Commission did not think it appropriate to recommend that a living will should cease to be effective in pregnancy. This is probably because a foetus is said to have no legal status (eg it was held in Re F[21] that a foetus cannot be made a ward of court) and has no right of action in English civil law and no existence independent of its mother. Thus a living will, which would have the effect, if implemented, of terminating the existence of a foetus, would appear to be valid.

This common law principle was queried in Re T[22] by Lord Donaldson, who suggested that a possible qualification on the right of a competent adult to choose or reject treatment was where such a choice might lead to the death of a viable foetus. In this case it was suggested that a pregnant woman cannot effectively refuse consent to life saving treatment at common law if this treatment is in the interests of both patient and foetus.

This line of argument was also adopted in the case of Re S[23] where a pregnant woman of 30 refused on religious grounds to consent to the carrying out of a caesarian section to assist in the birth of her baby. It was quite clear from the medical evidence that without the operation her baby could not be born alive and there was a serious risk to the mother's life. The president of the Family Division, Sir Stephen Brown held that the operation would be lawful without the mother's consent where the justification for overriding S's refusal of consent was that it was necessary to preserve the interests of the foetus.

It is difficult to reconcile these cases with the common law principle referred to above, that a foetus has no independent personality in law until the moment

---

21. *Re F (in utero) (wardship proceedings)* [1988] 2 FLR 307.

22. *Re T* [1992] 4 All ER 649.

23. *Re S* [1992] 4 All ER 671.

of birth. The decisions would suggest, however, that the effectiveness of a living will would be suspended during pregnancy if its effect were to cause the likely death of a foetus.

Conclusion

It has been argued that a living will is a 'white, middle-class approach to life planning which is at odds with how many people actually lead their lives, and may not even be the standard for that class'[24]. However, the living will clearly provides an important mechanism for involving people in decisions about their medical care which has become increasingly relevant as medical science has progressed. Further more it has been argued by Butler-Sloss LJ[25] that the widespread introduction of living wills in this country would be of great benefit both to the medical profession and to the courts. This is clearly an area which may become increasingly important to the health professional over the next few years.

---

24. King, P (1991) 'The Authority of Families to Make Medical Decisions for Incompetent Patients after the Cruzan Decision' Law, Medicine and Health Care 19, p 76
25. Butler-Sloss LJ (1994) in International Journal of Legal Education 28:2 p 125.

CASE STUDY ONE

Mr Brook, aged 45 years, executed a living will in contemplation of the possible onset of Alzheimer's disease, an illness from which both his parents had suffered. In his living will he declared that in the future he did not wish to be treated in order to prolong his life, 'if my mental state is so permanently impaired that there can be no likelihood of improvement'.

At the age of 52 Mr Brook was admitted to the long stay ward of a psychiatric hospital where he was diagnosed as suffering from an advanced form of Alzheimer's Disease. In accordance with his earlier expressed wishes he was not treated with antibiotics when he developed a chest infection, and he subsequently died.

Mrs Brook now wishes to sue the health authority for damages, on the grounds that the hospital staff were negligent in not treating her husband's respiratory infection, and that it was this negligence which caused his death.

The hospital respond by saying that as Mr Brook had executed a valid living will, they were entitled to rely on it, and thus were under no duty to treat the respiratory infection, and also that in any case Mr Brook's death was not caused by their failure to treat the patient, but by 'natural causes'.

Advise Mrs Brook.

CASE STUDY TWO

Jeremy, aged 15 years, is seriously injured in a coach crash. After six months it becomes clear that the brain damage he suffered is irreversible and he is diagnosed as being in a persistent vegetative state. He breaths unaided but needs to be fed through a naso-gastric tube. His mother wishes him to be allowed to 'die with dignity' but his father (who is estranged from Jeremy's mother) is adamant that he be kept alive 'at all costs'. Advise both parents as to the legal position.

9   Complaints, Coroners' Courts, Giving Evidence in Court

Complaints about hospital services

There are several methods of making a formal complaint about the quality of medical treatment which are distinct and separate from the process of litigation. The Hospital Complaints Procedures Act 1985 (which came into force in 1988) imposes a duty on the Health Minister to ensure that each hospital has arrangements for dealing with patients' complaints, and that those arrangements are adequately publicised. Often it would appear that a complainant simply requires a sympathetic ear and a reasonable explanation of events, and, if provided, this will often dispose of a complaint.

Complaints about hospital services, which should be received within three months of the event complained of (although there is latitude to accept late complaints) tend to fall into three categories:

- *environmental and support services*, which cover 'hotel' services and other facilities;

- *care*, which covers clinical and non clinical aspects from medical, para-medical and non-medical staff;

- *organisation*, which covers matters of general administration, including the handling of complaints.

There is no requirement that a complaint should be in writing, and if a complainant is unable to cater for himself, a friend or relative may act on his behalf.

Hospital complaints procedures regarding 'non clinical' matters

Formal complaints about hospital services which do not involve the exercise of clinical judgment are referred to the relevant District Health Authority or NHS Trust under the terms of HC88(37) which sets out directions issued by the Secretary of State under s 1 of the Hospital Complaints Procedures Act. Section 1(1) of the Act requires that:

(a)   ... arrangements are made for dealing with complaints made by or on behalf of persons who have been at (the relevant) hospital;

(b)   ... steps are taken for publishing the arrangements so made ...

HC(88)37 states that:

Patients are entitled to bring to the attention of Health Authorities aspects of their care and treatment about which they are unhappy. The Department recognises that suggestions, constructive criticism and complaints can be valuable aids to management in maintaining and developing better standards of health care. It is important that no one should be inhibited from making valid complaints and there is full confidence that these will be given proper and speedy consideration.

Publicity is required to be given to the complaints procedure adopted as this is an essential part of improving public perception; this is achieved by issuing information in the form of admission booklets, general leaflets and prominently displayed notices within the hospital. All hospital staff should know the name and location of the complaints officer and should receive training to ensure that they display positive attitudes towards patient complaints. A complainant must be notified in writing, as speedily as possible, of the results of the enquiry made by the complaints officer on his or her behalf.

Hospital complaints procedures: matters of clinical judgment

Complaints which concern the exercise of clinical judgment by hospital medical staff are dealt with under procedures set out in HC(81)5 and may, in the first instance, be made either to the consultant concerned or directly to the District Health Authority. In either case, at the initial stage, it is the responsibility of the consultant to examine the clinical aspects of the grievance and inform the district or unit manager of any significant risk of legal action.

If the complainant is dissatisfied with the consultant's reply he can be referred in writing to the Regional Medial Officer who will then try to resolve the complaint. If there is still no resolution of the problem the Regional Medical Officer may, at his discretion, arrange for a second opinion to be given by means of an Independent Professional Review (IPR) by two independent consultants. On completion of this review it is the responsibility of the district or general manager to inform the complainant of the result and of any action taken. The procedure offers no further remedy, however a complainant is not precluded from subsequent litigation.

It should be noted that complaints about clinical judgment do not come within the jurisdiction of the Health Services Commissioner (see below) , but the exercise of discretion by the Regional Medical Officer on whether to refer the complaint to IPR may be investigated by the Commissioner.

Health authorities are under a duty to monitor arrangements for dealing with complaints in order to identify trends and to direct that appropriate action is taken. Summaries of complaints must be provided at quarterly intervals for consideration whether by the authority itself, a committee of the authority, or by specified authority members.

Association of Community Health Councils

The Association of Community Health Councils in England and Wales was established under the National Health (Re-organisation) Act 1973; its members have statutory rights to, for example, visit the hospitals within the relevant district, be consulted on any substantial changes in local health care and be present and speak at meetings of the relevant health authority. Each ACHEW must publish an annual report to which the authority is required to make a detailed and specific reply.

ACHEW members also play a significant role in assisting complainants to bring their grievances to the attention of health authorities and the association has laid down five criteria for successful complaints handling[1]: visibility, accessibility, impartiality, effectiveness and speed. Most health authorities have gone some way to ensuring that these criteria are met, by the publication of leaflets, notices and admissions booklets which give information (in the appropriate languages) about complaints procedures; however, it would appear that only a small number of health authorities provide any special leaflet or training for staff on how to handle complaints or where to refer patients so that matters can be dealt with appropriately.

General Medical Council

The general accountability of doctors to the public is controlled by the General Medical Council, which oversees the training of doctors as well as issues relating to disciplinary proceedings arising from professional misconduct whether in the NHS or private practice; the Committee of the GMC may discipline a registered medical practitioner who has been convicted of a criminal offence or is guilty of 'serious professional misconduct'[2]. Serious professional misconduct may include serious neglect or disregard of responsibilities to patients, abuse of professional privilege in prescribing drugs or issuing medical certificates, abuse of professional confidence, abuse of the financial opportunities of medical practice, abuse of the doctor patient relationship and personal behaviour that could bring the profession into disrepute. A persistent criticism of the way that the GMC exercises its disciplinary powers is that it fails to deal with what would appear to be very unsatisfactory conduct, on the basis that it is not covered by the expression '*serious* professional misconduct'. The Medical (Professional Performance) Bill which is currently (August 1995) before Parliament and is expected to become law in late 1995 will extend the disciplinary powers of the

---

1. Association of Community Health Council in England and Wales (1990) *Hospital Complaints Procedures: a Review*, London ACHCEW.
2. Medical Act 1983 s 36; GMC's Guide to Professional Conduct and Discipline: Fitness to Practice, 1993.

GMC to cover doctors who have demonstrated a pattern of poor performance (that is, who are incompetent but whose single actions do not constitute 'serious professional misconduct'). The Labour Party advocated compulsory reaccreditation every seven years for doctors, but although this proposal has not been incorporated in the Bill, the government does support it[3].

Health Services Commissioner - the Ombudsman

Where patients do not feel that their complaint has been resolved satisfactorily the next step is to take the matter to the Health Services Commissioner whose powers are now set out in the National Health Service Act 1977 Part V. The Commissioner provides a service which is free to the complainant, is independent of the the NHS and government, and is accountable to Parliament. Complaints must be brought to the Commissioner's attention within one year of the matter for complaint arising.

Complainants must show that they have suffered injustice or hardship as a result of the failure in service, or from maladministration. Maladministration covers such matters as not following proper policies or agreed procedures, failing to have proper procedures, giving wrong information or inadequate explanations, or not dealing promptly or thoroughly with the original complaint.

Some of the main areas covered by the Commissioner in recent years have included the care of the mentally handicapped, the registration and supervision of private nursing homes, the operation of the clinical complaints procedure and the Family Health Service Authorities. Strictly speaking the Commissioner may not investigate a complaint where an aggrieved person has a right of appeal to an administrative tribunal or court of law. This requirement can be waived in appropriate cases.

The powers of the Commissioner are limited however, in that he may not deal with complaints where issues of clinical judgment are at stake, nor may he deal with a matter where the complainant has a remedy through the courts.

By far the largest number of complaints rejected by the Health Services Commissioner are those relating to clinical matters and that clearly involve issues of medical negligence for which a legal remedy is available.

Complaints against GPs

The Health Services Commissioner has no jurisdiction to investigate the actions of GP's in connection with services provided under contract with Family Health Service Authorities. (Note that some FHSA's have now merged with Regional Health Authorities and are now called Health Authorities and commissions.) Instead, complaints about family practitioners are dealt with by the relevant

---

3.   British Medical Association, 3 June 1995, Vol 310 p 1430.

FHSA under the provision of the Health Service (Service Committees and Tribunal Regulations) 1992 (SI 1992/664) by the relevant Medical Services Committee. Complaints against GP's are said to relate largely to alleged failures to diagnose and/or treat a patient competently, and failures to visit patients when requested.

Each FHSA must appoint an officer whose sole task (in contrast to health authorities) it is to deal with complaints. Depending on the nature of a complaint it may be dealt with either formally or informally.

In the *informal* procedure a negotiator is appointed by the FHSA who is usually a lay member of the FHSA; the lay negotiator will meet with the complainant in an effort to resolve the issue. If he is unsuccessful the complainant now has access to the full formal complaints procedure.

Formal investigation may only commence if the complaint is made within 13 weeks of the event complained of (or a longer period if the complainant can show good cause). The Chairman of the Service Committee will then determine whether there is a *prima facie* case against the doctor in question; if there is, the hearing will proceed, with both the complainant and the doctor representing themselves orally before the committee. The complainant is not entitled to legal aid or representation although he may ask a lawyer to help him prepare his case. No one other than the parties and the Committee members may be present at the hearing.

When the Service Committee has reached its conclusion regarding the complaint, a report is made to the FHSA who will decide if any action should be taken against the doctor concerned, and what that action should be; penalties against doctors range from a warning, to the withholding of remuneration to removal from the medical list. Both the complainant and the doctor concerned have the right to appeal against the decision of the medical committee to the Minister of Health (although at present the appeal actually lies to the Yorkshire Regional Health Authority, to whom appeals are delegated).

The coroner's court

A coroner has a duty to investigate every unnatural death by holding an inquest which is open to the public (except where national security is involved) and at which relatives and/or their legal representatives must be allowed to ask questions. Section 18 of the Coroners Act 1988 provides that the coroner need only have 'reasonable cause to suspect that the deceased has died an unnatural death' for him to have jurisdiction to hold the inquest.

As far as alleged acts of medical negligence which may have resulted in the death of a patient are concerned, the cost of the post mortem, the assimilation of evidence, the hearing and securing of witnesses' attendance and all other inquest costs will be borne by the state.

A coroner may be put on inquiry to investigate by any of the following persons:

- a registrar of births, deaths and marriages;

- medical practitioners;

- relatives;

- legal representatives;

- prison governors;

- police officers, etc.

A registrar of births deaths and marriages has a duty under r 51(i) of the Births, Deaths and Marriages Regulations 1968 to report a death to the coroner if the death is one:

(a) in respect of which the deceased was not attended during his last illness by a medical practitioner; or

(b) in respect of which the registrar has been unable to obtain a duly completed certificate of cause of death; or

(c) with respect to which it appears to the registrar, from the particulars contained in such a certificate or otherwise, that the deceased was seen by the certifying medical practitioner neither after death nor within 14 days before death; or

(d) the cause of which appears to be unknown; or

(e) which the registrar has reason to believe to have been unnatural or to have been caused by violence or neglect, or by abortion, or to have been attended by suspicious circumstances; or

(f) which appears to the registrar to have occurred during an operation or before recovery from the effect of an anaesthetic; or

(g) which appears to the registrar from the contents of any medical certificate to have been due to industrial disease or poisoning.

If the death is not reported by the doctor or the registrar because it is not, for example, considered to be 'unnatural' it is still open to a relative or his legal representative to draw the death to the coroner's attention because the death was 'at variance with what is natural, usual or to be expected'.

The coroner has a duty to make preliminary enquiries to determine if:

(a) he would have jurisdiction;

(b) his statutory duty to hold an inquest arises.

Section 19(1) of the Coroners Act 1988 provides a coroner with power to direct a *post mortem* without holding an inquest, if he is of the opinion that such an examination may prove an inquest unnecessary. However, a coroner does not have unrestricted power to hold an inquest in every case: 'It would be intolerable if he had the power to intrude without adequate cause ...' *R v Stephenson*[4]

The coroner is obliged by statute to hold an inquest if there is reasonable cause to suspect that the deceased has died:

(a) either a violent or an unnatural death;

(b) a sudden death the cause of which is unknown, and remains unknown following a post mortem examination;

(c) in prison;

(d) in such a place or under such circumstances as to require an inquest in pursuance of the Act.

Rule 6 of the Coroners Rules 1984 provides that where a person has sworn on oath before a coroner that, in that person's belief, the deceased's death was caused partly or entirely by the improper or negligent treatment of a medical practitioner, and the person has died in hospital:

the coroner should not direct or request a pathologist on the staff of, or associated with, that hospital to make a post mortem examination if:

(i)   the pathologist does not desire to make the examination, or

(ii)   the conduct of any member of the hospital staff is likely to be called in question, or

(iii) any relative of the deceased asks the coroner that the examination be not made by such a pathologist.

Rule 7 gives a relative the right to be informed as to where and when the post mortem is to take place and to have a right to be represented there by a doctor of their choice. Rule 19 gives a relative the right to be informed of the arrangements for the inquest; a legal representative who informs the coroner's office in advance of his interest in the proceedings similarly has a right to be informed.

The coroner has a duty to make a full and proper enquiry with the object of ascertaining (Coroners Rules 1984, r 36) who the deceased was, how, when and where he came by his death and the particulars for the time being required by the Registration Acts to be registered concerning the death.

If the coroner fails in his duty as set out above, the inquest can be quashed and a new one ordered under s 13(1) Coroners Act.

---

4.   *R v Stephenson* [1884] 13 QBD 331.

Proceedings in the coroner's court

From the moment an inquest is opened by the coroner, all rights of representation exist. Although in law it is not necessary formally to open and adjourn an inquest it is considered good practice as it constitutes a public pronouncement that a coroner's inquiry is taking place. A cremation certificate cannot be issued until an inquest is opened. There is no obligation placed on a coroner to release a list of witnesses which the parties intend to call, although legal representatives should ask for one as soon as possible. If a person whom it is considered relevant to call as a witness has not in fact been called, then a statement should be sent to the coroner outlining the reasons.

Interested parties have no right to advance disclosure of statements and documents relevant to the inquest although it is probable that the coroner has a legal duty to disclose the post mortem report as this would follow from the right to be represented at the inquest (Coroners Rules 1984 r 7). Not even bereaved relatives have a legal right to advance disclosure of documents (see *R v Hammersmith Coroner ex p Peach* [5]). The alleged reason for this rule is that the inquest is not an adversarial contest but rather is an inquisitorial process.

However, an application may be made to see the medical records of the deceased, and in *R v Southwark Coroner ex p Hicks*[6] a coroner who disregarded the requests of relatives, and refused to apply to the High Court for the issue of a *subpoena duces tecem* was subsequently criticised by the Court.

If the coroner is sitting alone he has no duty to sum up, however, if the coroner is sitting with a jury he must do so Coroners Rules 1984 r 41). He must direct the jury on issues of law as errors may lead to a successful application to have the verdict set aside. There is no legal aid available at inquests for the bereaved's representation.

Section 9 of the Contempt of Court Act 1981 provides that the press, public or legal representative may only bring a tape recorder into a court (including a coroner's court) at the coroner's discretion. A non-medically qualified coroner may sit with an assessor (eg a doctor) to assist him in his inquisitorial role, by indicating to him a useful line of questions.

An inquest is an enquiry to hear, by means of such evidence as is available, who the deceased was, and how and when he met his death. Hearsay evidence is therefore admitted in evidence. Documentary evidence will be admitted if, in the coroner's opinion, it is unlikely to be disputed. A relative will be entitled to a copy and may object to its admission.

---

5.   *R v Hammersmith Coroner ex parte Peach* [1980] 2 WLR 496.

6.   *R v Southwark Coroner ex p Hicks* [1987] 2 All ER 140.

The examination of witnesses is carried out under the provisions of the Coroners Rules 1984 r 20, which provides:

The coroner shall disallow any question which in his opinion is not relevant, or is otherwise not a proper question.

The rule against self-incrimination applies and in medical negligence cases where it is likely that the actions of any medical staff may also give rise to a prosecution for manslaughter, then Lord Denning's *dictum* in *Re Westinghouse Electric Corpn Uranium Contract Litigation*[7] will apply.

Once it appears that a witness is at risk, then great latitude should be allowed to him in judging for himself the effect of any particular question.

However, a witness cannot refuse to go into the witness box because he might incriminate himself. He can only claim privilege once sworn. The coroner has wide powers to get at the truth and a witness must appear and answer questions truthfully, or risk fine or imprisonment. Section 11(5) of the Coroners Act 1988 provides that an inquisition:

(a) shall be in writing under the hand of the coroner and in the case of an inquest held with a jury under the hands of the jurors who concur with the verdict;

(b) shall set out, so far as such particulars have been proved

(i) who the deceased was; and

(ii) how, when and where the deceased came by his death; and

(c) shall be in such form as the Lord Chancellor may by rules made by Statutory Instrument from time to time prescribe.

The Coroners Rules have 'suggested terms' for concluding how the deceased met his death, eg natural causes, accident. The term which is of particular interest in medical negligence cases is the 'accident/misadventure' alternative. The use of the misadventure verdict was criticised in *R v HM Coroner for Portsmouth ex parte Anderson*[8] where Mann J held that the meaning of 'misadventure' was indistinguishable from that of 'accident'. Except where there is a criminal element involved, eg unlawful killing, the civil standard of proof will apply *R v St Pancras Coroner's Court ex p Higgins* [9]).

Finally, the Coroners Rules 1984 r 43 provides that a coroner who believes that action should be taken to prevent the recurrence of fatalities similar to that in respect of which the inquest is being held, may announce at the inquest that

---

7. *Re Westinghouse Electric Corpn Uranium Contract Litigation* (No 2) [1977] 3 All ER 717.

8. *R v HM Coroner for Portsmouth ex p Anderson* [1987] 152 JP 56.

9. *R v St Pancras Coroner's Court ex p Higgins* [1988] 152 JP 637.

he is reporting the matter to the person or authority who may have power to take such action and he may report the matter accordingly.

Summoning a coroner's jury

A Coroner's jury must be summoned if the death in question occurred in prison (even if it was from natural causes); if the death occurred whilst the deceased was in police custody or resulted in an injury caused by a police officer in the purported execution of his or her duty; if the death was caused by an accident, poisoning or disease where notice is required to be given under statute to a government department and the coroner has decided to hold an inquest (he is not obliged to do so in all cases; for example, measles is a notifiable disease but if a sufferer dies 'naturally' from the disease then an inquest will not normally be held). Finally, the coroner must summon a jury if the death occurred in circumstances where there is a possibility of recurrence and the health and safety of the public may be prejudiced. As Bridge LJ said in *R v Hammersmith Coroner ex p Peach*:

> To take an example which was canvassed in the course of the argument, suppose a patient in a hospital dies from a mistaken injection of a drug in a fatal quantity, and suppose there is reason to suspect that that happened because the system operated in the hospital for the control, issue and handling of dangerous drugs is defective: This in my judgment ... would quite clearly be a circumstance of the kind contemplated in para (e) ...

Thus it is a matter for the coroner, properly directing himself, as to whether the circumstances bring the case within para (e) above. In any other circumstances the coroner has absolute discretion whether to summon a jury.

Giving evidence in court

It may be that nurses and other health professionals are required to give evidence in court, either at an inquest, or in the course of criminal or civil litigation. The advice given below is intended to assist in what may otherwise prove a worrying experience.

(a) It is better not to make any statement, either oral or written, in connection with court proceedings without informing your employer via your immediate line manager. Moreover you should take *professional* advice from a senior colleague and/or your professional body, and *legal* advice from your employer's legal adviser and your professional body before making any statement, either verbal or written.

(b) If it appears likely that you will have to attend court to give evidence, and you have never done so before, it is sensible to arrange to sit in on another case to gain experience. In any event you should always try to talk over the case with the lawyer who will be calling you to give evidence, beforehand.

(c) It is usual for a written statement (an affidavit) to be prepared in advance. In criminal cases the police will probably assist in helping you to draw up the statement. In civil cases you may well have to draw up the statement alone, perhaps with some assistance from your employer. Whatever the case, the statement should be as detailed as possible in relation to those issues which the court is likely to consider. Arrange the statement chronologically and under the following heads:

- name, qualifications, employer and nature of employment;

- first involvement with the patient involved in the case;

- details of all subsequent contacts with patient.

(d) Before giving evidence to the court you will be required to swear on oath (or affirm) that the evidence you are about to give will be truthful. You should address the Coroner as 'Sir', magistrates as 'Your Worship', judges in the county court or Crown Court as 'Your Honour' and judges in the High Court as 'My Lord'. You should also address all your remarks directly to the coroner, the bench or the judge, rather than to the lawyer who is asking you questions. Give your evidence in a slow, clear, audible voice which will enable the coroner, judge or magistrates to take longhand notes of your evidence if they so wish. If you wish to consult your written notes of the case, you must ask for the court's permission to do so by saying 'May I refer to my notes of the case Sir/My Lord/Your Honour/Your Worship?'

(e) It is likely that you will then be asked if the notes were made contemporaneously with, or as soon as possible thereafter, the events which they describe. If this is the case it is likely that you will be permitted to use them. The lawyer representing your side will know in advance, if he or she has prepared well for the case, what evidence you will give. Initial questions will be based on your written affidavit which will have been submitted in evidence.

(f) Questions asked in cross-examination may prove more difficult. Do *not* be rushed into giving an answer, or made to feel guilty about any lapse of memory. A pause for thought is acceptable. Remember that the court knows nothing at all about the case in advance, and the evidence of witnesses such as yourself is the means whereby the facts are identified. Always *explain* any medical terms that you use in evidence, and the significance of any professional observations that you make.

(g) Questions asked in cross-examination are designed to *test* the reliability of your evidence. Do not be upset or angry about this. The lawyer is only doing his job in presenting the best case possible for his client. Never be rushed into an incautious reply. It is perfectly acceptable to take time to think before replying. On the whole it is usually best to avoid straight 'yes' and 'no' answers, since it is unlikely that they represent the complete picture.

If you are asked questions which appear to be in breach of the UKCC Code of Professional Conduct on confidentiality issues, your first response should be to indicate this fact. Tell the court that to disclose confidential information about a patient's private life constitutes a breach of the professional code of conduct. There is plenty of case law which demonstrates that judges may respect professional confidence see *AG v Mulholland* and *Re D (Infants)*[10]. The court may then excuse you from answering, but if the court insists, then you must reply, or be guilty of contempt of court yourself. The cross-examination of a witness is intended to be penetrating, but should be carried out in a courteous manner. If the cross-examination is carried out aggressively, this will reflect badly on the other side, so stay calm.

(h) Once the cross-examination is concluded, the magistrate or judge may question the witness, and may then also give the witnesses' lawyer the opportunity to ask further questions. This is called re-examination.

No new evidence may be introduced in the re-examination, but it may give the witness the opportunity to set the record straight if it is felt that the cross-examination has lead to an incautious or otherwise unsatisfactory response.

(i) At the conclusion of the re-examination the witness is then asked to stand down from the witness box but is not free to leave the court until formally discharged since, in exceptional cases, it may prove necessary to re-call a witness.

---

10. *AG v Mulholland* [1963] 2 QB 477; *Re D (Infants)* [1970] 1 WLR 599.

CASE STUDY ONE

Mrs Jones is a patient on a long stay psychiatric ward; her behaviour is, at times, unpredictable and she has been known to be violent to other patients and staff. She is prescribed, on a regular basis, high doses of tranquilising medication which are administered by intra muscular injection. This makes her very drowsy and her relations are upset about the side effects of the medication. The ward doctor is however adamant that the medication is necessary.

Is there any action that Mrs Jones' relatives can take?

CASE STUDY TWO

Mr Singh was asked to attend the radiology department of his local hospital for a scan of his prostate gland. On arrival he was asked to wait, and, after three hours was eventually told to return home as the scanner was faulty. Mr Singh has taken the day off work without pay, and wishes to complain about the way that he was dealt with at the hospital and reimbursement for his lost wages.

To whom should Mr Singh complain, and what chance has he that his complaint will prove successful?

10   Medical Records

Introduction

Hospital medical records are the property of the employer, that is, the NHS trust or health authority. General practitioners' records are owned by the Family Health Services Authority. The law imposes on those personnel who have access to such records certain obligations. First there is a duty to ensure that the records are kept safely so that they are read only by authorised persons. A failure to take good care of such records could amount to a breach of the patient's right to confidentiality[1]. Furthermore, for health professionals who have a duty to make entries into those records a duty of care is owed to the patient to ensure their accuracy. Inaccurate statements may give rise to an action in negligence[2] or an action in defamation[3]. In addition, an employee who breaches his obligations in respect of those records could face disciplinary proceedings by his employer or even dismissal.

A case was reported in the *BMA News Review* about a patient who discovered that her medical records contained information about her alleged drug addiction. In fact she was not, and never had been, a drug addict and investigations revealed that another person had been using her name. The damage that this could have caused her was potentially enormous.

Maintenance and storage of medical records

The Department of Health recommends[4] that medical records be stored for minimum periods of time; personal health records should be kept for at least eight years, obstetric records for 25 years and those relating to the mentally ill for at least 20 years. The employer clearly has an interest in ensuring that records are appropriately stored for this length of time as they may be needed to defend an action in negligence which could conceivably take place many years after the alleged negligent act took place[5]. It is also imperative that full, accurate and legible records are maintained. There are many cases (mostly involving claims

---

1. See Chapter 11 on confidentiality.
2. See Chapter 1 on medical negligence.
3. Doctors and Defamation, Legal Correspondent [1985] 290 BMJ 1342.
4. Department of HC(80)7.
5. Limitation Act 1980.

against doctors but they have implications for nurses too) where the records have been inadequate for the purposes of subsequent litigation[6].

Limitation periods

The Limitation Act 1980[7] requires that a writ for a claim arising from personal injury be served within three years from either the date of the negligent treatment or the 'date of knowledge' whichever is the later. It is this latter concept which has proved to be less than straightforward. To be successful in a claim made more than three years after the accident a plaintiff must be able to prove that he served the writ within three years of establishing the link between the injury suffered and the event which caused the injury. A good example is provided by the following case[8]:

In 1977 the plaintiff underwent a mammography which was subsequently proved to have been conducted negligently. For eight years she was repeatedly assured that the symptoms she suffered could not have been caused by the X-ray until in 1985 the necessary link was established. She issued her writ in February 1988 claiming damages for personal injury, which by then was over ten years after the negligent act but within the necessary three years of her gaining the requisite 'knowledge'. Her belief that she had been a victim of negligence at the time was held by the court to be insufficient to exclude her from the protection of the legislation.

In addition to this provision the courts have discretion to allow 'late' claims to succeed where in all the circumstances it is fair to the parties to do so[9]. The courts, in exercising this discretion, will take into account the conduct of the parties after the cause of action arose, the length and reasons for the delay and its effect on the available evidence.

If the victim is under 18 years of age or of 'unsound mind' within the provisions of the Mental Health Act 1983 at the time the negligent act takes place, the Limitation Act 1980[10] allows him to sue within three years of the disability ending. Thus for a child who is injured in a medical accident the three years will run from his 18th birthday unless, at this point in time he is deemed to be of 'unsound mind, eg as a result of a brain damage. In such cases the disability presumably will not end until death and thus the three years would run from

---

6. See, eg *Fiennes v McEwan* [1985] 18 October QB (unreported).
7. Section 11.
8. *Steven v Riverside Health Authority* (1989) *The Times* 5 December.
9. Limitation Act 1980, s 33.
10. Section 28.

that event. In practice, however, a parent or guardian will usually bring the action as 'next friend' much earlier.

It is important to remember that these rules only apply to the service of the writ. Once started, an action can take many years before it is either settled out of court (as the vast majority are) or the court passes judgment.

Patients' access to health records

At common law a patient had no right of access to medical records. Legislation has now intervened and access is available under the following statutes.

The Data Protection Act 1984

A growing number of medical records are today kept on computer. Under the Act where information is kept on computer which relates to a person who can be identified from that information, the 'data user', that is, the person/s who controls the contents and use of the data (normally the employer) has certain statutory obligations. One important obligation is that the 'data subject', that is, the person on whom the information is kept, must be provided access to that data. If requested the information must be supplied to the 'subject' in a form in which it can be understood, and within a reasonable time (usually 40 days). Thus a patient can request, on payment of a small fee, any records kept by a hospital or general practitioner on data base.

The Act does, however, allow access to be refused in certain circumstances. Thus, if a health professional feels that the information is likely to cause serious harm to the physical or mental health of the patient who is requesting access, that information can be withheld[11]. Further, if access would reveal the identity of another individual (other that a health care professional), and that other person does not wish his identity to be revealed, then again disclosure can be refused. Under the Data Protection (Subject Access Modification) (Health) Order 1987[12] where the 'data user' is not a health professional (eg a hospital manager), information must not be divulged without first consulting the relevant health professional (eg doctor, nurse, dentist, etc). It is worth noting that the duty under the regulations is to consult only, and advice can be ignored!

A patient (or any other data subject) who is refused access by a data user has a right to challenge this refusal in the county court[13]. If an individual suffers damage by reason of any inaccuracy in his data records, the Act gives that per-

---

11. The Access to Health Records Act 1990 has the same exceptions and they are discussed more fully with reference to that Act.

12. SI 1987/1903.

13. Data Protection Act 1984, s 21(8).

son a right to claim compensation for damage and distress. It is a defence, however, to such a claim if the data user can prove that he took 'such care as in all the circumstances was reasonably required to ensure the accuracy of the data at the material time'[14]. A court can order the rectification or erasure of any inaccurate information[15]. The Act also allows for payment of compensation in the event that the information is disclosed to a third party without the authority of the subject[16].

The Access to Medical Reports Act 1988

This Act gives a patient the right to see a copy of a medical report (on payment of a reasonable fee) which has been requested for insurance or employment purposes before it is sent. In addition, the Act gives a patient the right to correct any errors which the report might contain (or if the doctor refuses, to append a statement to the report setting out the objections) and to withhold consent to it being sent. If the patient (who must be informed of his right of access) indicates that he wishes to see the report, the doctor must wait 21 days before sending it. If during that time no objection is made then the report can be supplied.

Again the legislation allows a doctor to withhold access if, in his opinion, the report is likely to cause serious harm to the physical or mental health of the patient or third parties, or would reveal the identity of a third party (other than a health professional involved in the care of that individual) without his consent.

Complaints about breach of any of the provisions of the Act are heard in the county court.

Access to Health Records Act 1990

This statute was enacted after the failure of the medical profession to develop a voluntary code of practice regarding patients' access to their medical records. Its aim is to ensure greater accuracy in record keeping by doctors, and to give patients an earlier indication of potential causes of action.

Under the Act patients are given a statutory right to obtain access to their personal health records, thus extending the existing statutory rights to information provided under the Data Protection Act 1984 and the Access to Medical Reports Act 1988 outlined above. The Act came into force on 1 November 1991.

The Act applies to all 'health records', ie information relating to the physical and mental health of an individual (s 1) made by, or on behalf of, a health pro-

---

14. Section 22(3).
15. Section 24.
16. Section 23.

fessional in connection with the care of the individual. The term health professional used in s 2 covers the patient's:

- registered medical practitioner;

- dentist;

- optician;

- chemist;

- registered nurse;

- midwife;

- health visitor;

- chiropodist;

- physiotherapist;

- speech therapist;

- clinical psychologist; and

- a scientist employed by a health authority or other NHS body.

The patient, the patient's appointee or personal representative and the patient's parent (where the patient is a child) may all apply for access under the Act. Where the patient is a child, and the application is made by his parent or representative, the holder of the health records must be satisfied that the child has consented to the application. If the child is unable to consent because of lack of understanding, the holder must ensure that the access would be in the patient's 'best interests' before the records are released (s 4(2)).

Access to a deceased person's record is not granted if the record contains a note that the deceased patient did not wish access to be granted after his death (s 4(3)).

Application is made to the holder who is usually the relevant medical practitioner or health authority, who must grant access within 21 days (if the record was made within 40 days immediately preceding the date of application), or within 40 days of the date of application. Under s 3(4), a fee (currently £10) is chargeable if the entire contents of the records applied for were made more than 40 days prior to the application.

If the applicant requires a copy of the records to be made, the actual cost of photocopying and posting may be charged. The holder may be required by the applicant to explain records where meaning (or handwriting) unclear.

The holder of health records may refuse access where:

- in the opinion of the practitioner disclosure would be likely to cause 'serious harm' to the physical or mental health of the patient or of a third party (see similar provisions in the Data Protection Act 1984); or

- information recorded in the health record has been provided by an individual other than the patient or the health care professional to whom application is made, that individual's consent must be obtained prior to disclosure; or

- the relevant records were made prior to 1 November 1991, unless access to such records is necessary to explain post-Act entries (s 5). In *R v Mid-Glamorgan FHSA ex p Martin* (1993)[17] the High Court confirmed that a patient does not have a right of access to his health record prior to the Act coming into force.

It is important to note that the Act confers upon the holder of the health record the right to judge whether a record is inaccurate, or is likely to cause serious harm to the patient if disclosed.

Examples of situations where disclosure might be refused are limited. The general principle is that if the health record contains information that the patient is suffering from a serious condition, eg cancer, and access has been requested, then the patient must generally accept the consequences. The more likely reason for refusal to provide access is where third party identity is in issue. Thus a health record which contains information given by, eg a spouse to a doctor or nurse about the fears the spouse has concerning the patient's behaviour cannot be disclosed without that spouse's consent.

Where a patient considers that his health records contain information which is incorrect, misleading or incomplete he may apply to the holder for a correction to be made, but there is no absolute right to secure correction. The patient must be provided with evidence of any correction made at his request. If the health professional refuses to correct the records, then the patient has the right to append to his notes a copy of his objections, and the holder must furnish the patient with evidence that this has been done.

Where a patient fails to obtain access (either because the holder believes he has a statutory right to refuse, or because of dilatoriness on the part of the holder) application may be made to the county court or the High Court for an order requiring the holder to comply with his obligations under the Act.

---

17. *R v Mid-Glamorgan FHSA ex p Martin* (1993) *The Times* 2 June.

CASE STUDY ONE

Mr Evans, a regular visitor to the Health Centre, consults the practice nurse whom he has been seeing over a period of days for replacement dressings to a wound he received to his arm in a public house brawl. Mrs Evans and his three children, aged 10, 8 and 5 are patients at the same practice. Mr Evans, who is unemployed, is alleged by his wife to have physically and mentally abused both her and the children, and is suspected of having a 'drink problem'. The nurse knows that there are various references to all these things in his medical records (assume the entries have been made after 1 November 1991). The records also contain letters from the Social Services Department, the NSPCC and a psychiatrist to whom he was recently referred. In addition a neighbour of the family called at the surgery last month to express her concern about Mr Evans and the risk which she thought he presented to the family. She was advised to contact the NSPCC and the police. An entry relating to this also appears.

Mrs Evans eventually makes application to the court for an injunction to remove Mr Evans from the matrimonial home (a council tenancy) alleging that both she and the children are at serious risk of harm. Mr Evans strongly denies this and he wants both the nurse and the doctor to provide him with a medical report and character reference to submit to the court so that he can 'properly defend myself against this vicious attack'. He demands immediate access to his own health records, his wife's and his children's to make sure that they do not contain 'scurrilous lies about me'.

Must he be granted access?

CASE STUDY TWO

Bertha is a 48 year old woman who, over the past six months, presented to her GP complaining, *inter alia*, of the following symptoms:

* general malaise and lethargy, lack of ability to concentrate;
* general discomfort of the abdomen;
* increased pain on menstruation;
* fainting attacks;
* phlebitis.

At the earlier consultation the GP expressed some sympathy and concern, undertaking at least some basic physical examinations. He diagnosed the menopause. As time went by the records demonstrate an erosion of goodwill, and the later comments include 'over-anxious', 'malingerer', 'wasting my time', etc.

Within a few days of her last consultation, Bertha was admitted to the local general hospital where she underwent emergency surgery for ovarian cancer. Both she and her husband are informed of the diagnosis and, in passing the consultant gynaecologist mentioned that 'it was a pity that we could not have caught it earlier'.

Bertha's husband wishes to see his wife's GP records so that he can gauge whether the doctor has been negligent. Bertha will give her consent to any application. Must access in these circumstances be granted?

CASE STUDY THREE

Carlos Gonzales, a 65 year old patient suffering from lung cancer, is admitted to hospital suffering from pneumonia and cardiac failure. Recorded in his nursing and medical notes is a 'do not resusitate order'. A week after admission Carlos suffers a cardiac arrest, the 'crash team' are not called and Carlos dies.

Carlos' widow is extremely distressed – she had not been informed that her husband was suffering from lung cancer despite the fact that the diagnosis had been made six months previously. Nor was she told about the decision not to resuscitate. She feels that not enough was done to keep her husband alive and is demanding a copy of her husband's records 'to take to my solicitor'. The nursing notes record, *inter alia*, the following:

'Mrs Gonzales is an irritating and demanding woman, constantly criticising the medical and nursing staff. She should be discouraged from visiting Carlos so frequently as she is upsetting the ward routine and exacerbating Carlos' own anxious state.'

If disclosure is made would Mrs Gonzales have a cause of action in law in respect of any (or all) of the following:

- the 'do not resuscitate order';

- the entry describing her as 'irritating and demanding';

- the failure to inform her of her husband's condition.

CASE STUDY FOUR

Deirdre, a 39 year old mother of five children, is admitted to hospital for a termination of pregnancy and sterilisation. On admission she is asked to sign a standard consent form which she willingly does.

The next day, shortly after receiving her 'pre-med' she tells the nurse that she no longer wishes to go ahead with the sterilisation though she is happy to have the termination. The nurse communicates this information to the doctor who is unsympathetic and informs the nurse that he is unwilling to undertake a termination without performing the sterilisation because in his opinion 'Deirdre is socially inadequate and incapable of caring for the ones she has got'. By the time this information is relayed to Deirdre she is feeling extremely drowsy. The operation goes ahead and the next day, when Deirdre learns that the sterilisation has been performed she becomes hysterical and threatens legal action.

If Deirdre asks for a copy of her notes, what should she expect to see recorded there in respect of the details outlined above?

Would Deirdre have a cause of action against the doctor, the nurse, or any other person or body?

11 Confidentiality, Patients and the Law

Background

A health care professional's duty to maintain his patient's confidentiality is well documented. A doctor's obligation is enshrined in such statements as, 'The doctor owes to his patient complete loyalty; a doctor shall preserve absolute secrecy on all he knows about his patient because of the confidence entrusted in him'[1] and 'I will respect the secrets which are confided in me even after the patient has died'[2]. In addition the General Medical Council's 'Blue Book'[3], drawn up in pursuance of the Medical Act 1983, s 35 contains strict rules which oblige a doctor to refrain from third party disclosure of information obtained in a professional capacity. This duty of confidentiality is similarly recognised by the courts in this country both as a general principle[4] and in relation specifically to doctors; '... the doctor is under a duty not to (voluntarily) disclose, without the consent of the patient, information which he, the doctor, has gained in his professional capacity'[5].

The same principles apply to nurses and other medical personnel. A similar provision to the GMC Blue Book is incorporated in the UKCC Code of Practice which states that:

> as a registered nurse, midwife or health visitor, you are personally accountable for your practice and, in the exercise of your professional accountability, must:

> protect all confidential information concerning patients and clients obtained in the course of professional practice and make disclosures only with consent, where required by the order of the court or where you can justify disclosure in the wider public interest[6].

---

1. The International Code of Medical Ethics.
2. Declaration of Geneva.
3. 'Professional Conduct and Discipline: Fitness to Practice' GMC February 1993.
4. *A-G v Guardian Newspapers Ltd (No 2)* [1990] 1 AC 455.
5. *Hunter v Mann* [1974] QB 767.
6. UKCC Code of Professional Conduct, June 1992 para 9.

Exceptions to the duty of confidentiality

The duty of confidentiality is thus not absolute; the UKCC, as indicated above, the GMC and the courts recognise certain important exceptions to this duty. A UKCC Advisory Paper on Confidentiality expands on the basic obligation provided for in the Code of Practice.

1. A patient/client has a right to expect that information given in confidence will be used only for the purpose for which it was given and will not be released to others without their consent.

2. That practitioners recognise the fundamental right of their patients/clients to have information about them held in secure and private storage.

3. That, where it is deemed appropriate to share information obtained in the course of professional practice with other health or social work practitioners, the practitioner who obtained the information must ensure, as far as is reasonable, before its release that it is being imparted in strict professional confidence and for a specific purpose.

4. That the responsibility either to disclose or withhold confidential information in the public interest lies with the individual practitioner, that he or she cannot delegate the decision, and that he or she cannot be required by a superior to disclose or withhold information against his or her will.

5. That a practitioner who chooses to breach the basic principle of confidentiality in the belief that it is necessary in the public interest must have considered the matter sufficiently to justify that decision.

6. That deliberate breaches of confidentiality other than with the consent of the patient/client should be exceptional.

   The important exceptions are considered in turn.

Where the patient consents to disclosure

Positive consent to the release of information by the patient clearly exempts a nurse or doctor from his obligation of confidentiality[7]. However, such disclosure is limited to the scope of this consent, that is, for the purposes which have been explained to the patient. Consent to disclosure may, however, also be implied so that, for example, while a patient may not have given express consent to the nurse to impart information about his condition to the next of kin, the right to do this would be implied unless instructions had been given to the contrary. It is also recognised that the medical profession are permitted to share

---

7. *C v C* [1946] 1 All ER 562.

a patient's information with colleagues responsible for the clinical management of the patient although a doctor or nurse has a positive duty to ensure that such professionals are in no doubt that the information is confidential. The GMC also now imposes on doctors a 'responsibility to ensure that arrangements exist to inform patients of the circumstances in which information about them is likely to be shared and the opportunity to state any objections to this'[8].

Where it is in the best interests of the patient to disclose

If a doctor or nurse decides, in exercise of his clinical judgment, to disclose information about her patient without consent, or because the patient cannot be judged capable of giving consent, then disclosure may take place but such a person 'must be prepared to explain and justify that decision, whatever the circumstances of the disclosure'. A child patient suspected of being a victim of child abuse serves as a good illustration. If there existed in this country a requirement for compulsory reporting of suspected child abuse as exists in the US, Canada and some states of Australia, the problem about disclosure would be overcome.

A more difficult problem relating to disclosure arises for the medical profession in relation to under age patients' sexual activities. It is now established[9] that a child under 16 may be competent to consent to medical treatment (including contraception) and it would arguably therefore directly follow from this that such a competent patient would enjoy the right to confidentiality. However, would a doctor or nurse who disclosed to parents of such a child that child's request for contraception or indeed a termination of pregnancy, be held guilty of 'serious professional misconduct' by the Professional Conduct Committee of the GMC or the UKCC? In a case before the GMC in 1971[10] a doctor was held not guilty of serious professional misconduct when he divulged to parents of a 16 year old child that she was using contraceptive medication. It is certainly arguable that the PCC would reach a different decision today both because of the *Gillick* decision[11] and because it would contravene the spirit of the Children Act 1989 which makes the child's welfare paramount and replaces the concept of parental 'rights and duties' with that of 'parental responsibility'.

Where disclosure is in the public interest

There are cases where the desire to preserve the confidential relationship which exists between the medical professional and his patient must be subordinated to

---

8. 'Guidance for Doctors on Professional Confidence' GMC November 1991.
9. *Gillick v West Norfolk and Wisbech Area Health Authority* [1986] AC 112.
10. *GMC v Browne* (1971) *The Times* 6 and 8 March.
11. See n 7.

the duty which is cast on every good citizen to assist in the investigation of serious crime[12].

The GMC explains public interest disclosure by reference to the exposure of 'a patient, or someone else, to a risk of death or serious harm'[13]. Public interest is, however, a difficult concept to define. If a patient or client admits to a nurse that he has just killed his partner, it would be difficult for that patient to argue subsequently that the nurse was not justified in informing the police. Most cases are not, however, so clear cut. Neither a nurse or doctor has any legal obligation to divulge confidential information to the police. If information is divulged then the nurse would be required to make a statement. If in doubt, advise from senior staff should be sought.

The leading case in this area is now *W v Egdell*[14]; a consultant psychiatrist was asked for an independent report by the patient's solicitor in support of his application to a Mental Health Review Tribunal for release or transfer from a secure unit in which he was detained as a result of killing five people. The report which was later submitted was unfavourable to the patient and the case was subsequently withdrawn from the tribunal. However, the psychiatrist knew that the patient's case would be considered automatically by the tribunal in the near future and the psychiatrist feared that his report would be unavailable to them. He therefore sent a copy of the report to the Home Office and the psychiatrist in charge of the secure unit. In an action for damages for breach of contract (the relationship between doctor and patient was here a contractual one as the psychiatrist in question had been contracted to provide a report by the patient's solicitor) and in equity alleging breach of a duty of confidence the Court of Appeal held that, while the duty of confidentiality clearly arose from the relationship, the fear of a real risk to public safety entitled a doctor to take reasonable steps to communicate his grounds for concern.

The serious risk involved in this case was clear justification for the court's decision. What, though, of the doctor whose patient has become unfit to drive through illness or age but fails to report his disability or consent to its disclosure? It is likely that a doctor is protected from any action for breach of confidence if a report is made to the medical authorities of the vehicle licensing centre. However, it is almost certain that the GMC and UKCC would look unfavourably if disclosure were made to non-medical third parties (eg insurers).

Disclosure of a patient's medical history and current mental condition without consent might also be justified in adoption proceedings where a mother refuses or withdraws consent to an application to the court for an adoption

---

12. Aver, J Birmingham Assizes [1914] 78 JP 604.

13. Paragraph 11.

14. *W v Egdell* [1990] 1 AC 109.

order to be made. In a recent case[15] where a court was asked to exclude evidence submitted to it as a result of a doctor allegedly breaching her patient's confidentiality by divulging the patient's medical condition to support an application from prospective adoptive parents for an adoption order, the doctor justified her decision on the grounds that, in her opinion, the child's interests would be better protected if an adoption order was made. This opinion was supported by the Court of Appeal where it was said by Stuart-Smith LJ 'The adoption of a child is a matter of very great public importance. It affects the welfare of the child for the rest of its life ...' and 'I am by no means satisfied that in the circumstances of this case there was any breach of that duty in disclosing these matters to those who were concerned with the welfare of the child, namely the court and the solicitors of the adopters'. The evidence given by the doctor was therefore held admissible though the case is not authority for a general principle that disclosure in these circumstances falls within the permitted exceptions to the principles outlined above as the court was not being asked to rule on this issue specifically. Neither can we necessarily predict the response of the GMC if a complaint based on similar facts were ever lodged with them.

The public interest in disclosure versus the private right to have one's confidences protected is probably most keenly felt in AIDS-related cases. In a recent case where a health authority sought an injunction against a newspaper to restrain the publication of information which had been improperly disclosed (the names of two doctors who were being treated for AIDS) the judge said:

> The public in general, and patients in particular, are entitled to expect hospital records to be confidential and it is not for any individual to take it upon himself or herself to breach that confidence whether induced by a journalist or otherwise[16].

This is a clear indication that private rights prevail in these circumstances over what was recognised by the court in this case as a 'genuine public interest'.

The GMC advises that if a patient with HIV refuses to consent to disclosure, even to his general practitioner, this refusal should be respected unless there is a real risk to health care staff if disclosure is not made[17]. Could disclosure be made to the patient's sexual partner(s) without consent? Such disclosure would certainly amount to a breach of confidentiality but it is probable (although there is as yet no legal authority on this point) that the courts and the GMC and UKCC would regard such disclosure as justifiable, given the possible fatal consequences.

Does a doctor, nurse or other health care professional, have a positive duty to warn any patient of his of the risks attendant on maintaining (or establishing)

---

15. *Re (C) A Minor* [1991] FCR 553.

16. *X (Health Authority) v Y* [1988] 2 All ER 648.

17. 'HIV Infection and Aids: The Ethical Considerations' GMC 1988.

a sexual relationship with another patient whom the doctor knows is HIV positive, that is, can liability ever arise from a failure to divulge confidential information? In the US and some Canadian provinces there is a statutory duty to warn and a failure to so warn has given rise to successful actions in damages[18]. In this country there is no commensurate statutory duty but it is arguable that a doctor's failure to warn of the risks in these circumstances could give rise to a liability in negligence on the basis that the doctor owed his patient at risk of being infected a duty of care[19]. Again there is no authority and the medical profession might feel better protected if the law in this area was made clearer.

Disclosure in connection with legal proceedings

Doctors and nurses, unlike solicitors, do not have a defence of privilege in relation to their clients' confidences and therefore a doctor or nurse who refuses to obey an order of the court requiring disclosure would be in contempt of court. Therefore, the failure to provide information which may lead to the identification of a driver involved in a road traffic accident as required by the Road Traffic Act 1988, s 172 would give rise to liability[20] as would a refusal to supply information required under the Prevention of Terrorism Act 1989, s 18. Various other statutes provide for, *inter alia*, the reporting of infectious diseases[21], reporting for statistical purposes[22], public protection purposes[23] and reporting deaths to coroners[24]. A court, similarly, can order disclosure of medical records in connection with, eg medical negligence litigation[25].

Disclosure for the purposes of medical research

Disclosure for the purpose of a medical research project may take place if the project has been approved by a recognised ethical committee. A nurse (or hospital doctor) taking part in a research project should, as an employee, obtain permission from the hospital management. The GMC states that, because medical teaching, research and medical audit will, of necessity, involve the disclosure of information about individuals:

> where disclosure would enable one or more individuals to be identified, the patients concerned, or those who may properly give permission on their behalf, must wherever possible

---

18. *Tarasoff v Regents of the University of California* [1976] 131 Cal Rptr 14.

19. *Bolam v Friern Hospital Management Committee* [1957] 2 All ER 118.

20. *Hunter v Mann* [1974] QB 767.

21. Public Health (Infectious Diseases) Regulations 1988, SI 1988/1546.

22. Abortion Regulations 1968, SI 1968/390.

23. Misuse of Drugs (Notification of and Supply to Addicts) Regulations, 1973 SI 1973/799.

24. Coroners Act 1988.

25. Supreme Court Act 1981, s 33.

be made aware of that possibility and be advised that it is open to them, at any stage, to withhold their consent to disclosure[26].

Remedies

A doctor or nurse who breaches his duty of confidentiality could clearly face disciplinary proceedings before the GMC's Professional Conduct Committee or UKCC and a serious breach could lead to erasure from the register. A patient may also lodge a complaint under the Hospital Complaints Procedure Act 1985 if the unlawful disclosure had been made by a hospital doctor or nurse. In these circumstances the doctor or nurse might face disciplinary proceedings by his employing health authority who would have the right to dismiss for serious breaches. Similarly, complaints against general practitioners or practice nurses could be made to the Family Health Services Authority who also act as a disciplinary body.

Whether a patient can recover damages for an unlawful breach of confidence by a medical professional is in some cases uncertain. If the information disclosed is untrue then an action in damages for defamation would certainly lie[27]. In the absence of a defamation claim, damages may be irrecoverable. There is no decided case where a claim for damages for breach of confidentiality has been successful other than in relation to a commercial claim[28] although some literature assumes that such a cause of action does exist. Most of the case law on breach of confidentiality relates to claims for injunctions to restrain threatened breaches of confidentiality[29] and it is clear that a doctor or nurse in such circumstances could be served with an injunction preventing disclosure. However, injunctions, once disclosure has been made, are clearly of little value and, apart from being entitled to enact the various procedures outlined above, a patient may have no further redress.

---

26. 'Professional Conduct and Discipline: Fitness to Practice' GMC 1993.

27. *Kitson v Playfair* (1986) *The Times* 28 March.

28. *Seager v Copydex* [1967] 1 WLR 923.

29. See eg *Argyll v Argyll* [1967] Ch 302.

CASE STUDY ONE

Jasmine is two years old and is admitted to the children's hospital with a fractured furmur and suspected fracture of the skull. Her mother tells the nurse on duty that Jasmine had fallen off a slide in the local playground. Subsequent observation of the mother with Jasmine leads the nursing staff to suspect that Jasmine is in fact a victim of a non-accidental injury.

What should the nursing staff do and what issues of confidentiality arise?

CASE STUDY TWO

Mrs James is a patient on an acute ward who has just been diagnosed as suffering from ovarian cancer. She is estranged from her husband and made it clear to the nurse on admission that she did not wish her husband to be informed of any of the details about her illness. One day Mr James arrives in the ward and questions the nurse on duty about his wife's prognosis. Although the nurse is reluctant to talk in any detail about Mrs James' illness, Mr James does, unwittingly, extract from the nurse the medical view that her prognosis is poor.

Can Mrs James take action against the nurse and/or the hospital?

CASE STUDY THREE

Two nurses were standing at the bus stop discussing the fact that Mrs Jones, a patient on their ward, had just been diagnosed as suffering from carcinoma of the breast. The conversation was overheard, unknown to the nurses, by Mrs Jones' next door neighbour who was able to identify the patient from the conversation.

What legal and ethical issues arise as a result of this?

CASE STUDY FOUR

Mr Doe is brought to casualty obviously suffering from the effects of having been involved in a particularly vicious fight. The police arrive an hour later and demand to see him. He is totally unco-operative with them but had, on admission, given the nursing staff all the usual personal details. The police are now demanding that they be informed of his name, address, next of kin and the exact location of where the ambulance picked him up.

Is there a legal and/or moral duty to divulge this information?

CASE STUDY FIVE

Mr Smith is a 42 year old well built and athletic man. Out of the blue he appeared to suffer an epileptic fit and was admitted to hospital where various investigations were carried out. As a result he was diagnosed as suffering from a malignant cerebral tumour and his wife was told by the doctors that he had no more than three months to live. The wife instructed the doctor not to tell her husband.

A decision was made to give radiotherapy as a palliative measure and when Mr Smith was asked to consent to the treatment it was explained to him that it was necessary to prevent him having a further 'fit'. As a result he gave his consent.

What legal and ethical issues arise from this?

CASE STUDY SIX

Ms Brown, a registered general nurse was off duty, doing her shopping. She witnessed a road traffic accident and went to give assistance until the ambulance arrived. The injured person was left with a permanent disability and later sued Ms Brown alleging that his injuries were caused by her inappropriate treatment.

What are the legal and ethical issues at stake here?

12 Liability of Health Authorities and NHS Trusts

Vicarious liability – basic principles

The basic common law principle is that an employer is liable for the negligent acts or omissions committed by his employee in the course of employment; this is known as 'vicarious liability'. The employer's liability for his employees' acts does not relieve the employee of liability to the plaintiff, who may seek compensation from either or both parties. However except in very limited circumstances an employer is not vicariously liable for the negligent acts or omissions of an independent contractor, provided he can prove that due care was shown in the selection of the contractor. This principle applies equally to the provision of health care; a health authority or NHS charitable trust may be held to be vicariously liable for the acts of its negligent employees, provided they are carried out in the course of employment.

Although a plaintiff who claims he was injured by the negligence of a doctor or nurse will retain a right of action against that individual, there are undoubted advantages in suing the health authority or NHS trust that employs him. The employer will normally have a 'deeper pocket' than the employee, or will have insured against the risk, and is thus more attractive as a defendant. Moreover there will be circumstances where a patient may be unable to identify exactly which members of the medical team that treated him committed the negligent act or acts which caused his injury and thus will not be able to name an individual defendant. In these circumstances it is clearly more desirable to sue the employer.

General practitioners

It is now thought that a health authority is not vicariously liable for the negligent acts of general practitioners since there is no contract between them, although for some time the nature of the legal relationship was not clear. There were apparently conflicting decisions in *Wadi v Cornwall and Isles of Scilly FPC*[1] (which held that there was no contractual relationship between the parties) and the Court of Appeal decision in *Roy v Kensington and Chelsea FPC*[2] (which held that there was). These difficulties appear to have been finally resolved by the House of Lords in *Roy*[3] where Lord Bridge commented:

---

1. *Wadi v Cornwall and Isles of Scilly FPC* [1985] 1 ICR 492.
2. *Roy v Kensington and Chelsea FPC* [1990] 1 Med LR 328.
3 *Roy* [1992] AC 624 HL.

I do not think the issue in the appeal depends upon whether the doctor provides services pursuant to a contract with the Family Practitioner Committee. I doubt if it does and am content to assume that *there is no contract*. (Emphasis added.)

Thus a GP will be personally liable for his own negligent acts, however, if he is a member of a partnership he may be jointly responsible for the negligent acts of his partners, and if it is not the doctor himself but rather an employee (eg practice nurse) who has been negligent the GP may be vicariously liable for the acts of that employee. Thus a doctor would be vicariously liable for the negligence of a practice nurse or receptionist, providing it could be proved that their negligent acts, had actually caused the injury complained of by the patient (see Chapter 1).

Where a GP uses a *locum* (or a deputising service) to act on his behalf he will not be vicariously liable for any negligent acts of the *locum*. However if a plaintiff can show that the doctor failed to exercise due care in the selection of the *locum* this may amount to a breach of his duty of care to the patient, in which case he will be personally liable.

Vicarious liability of health authorities and hospitals

The original common law position was that hospitals and health authorities were not vicariously liable for the negligent acts of their professionally qualified staff. Thus, in 1906[4] it was held that a hospital was not vicariously liable for the negligence of a doctor employee because, in this special type of employment, the hospital did not have sufficient control over the doctor as to the manner of the performance of his professional duties. Similarly in *Hillyer v St Bartholomew's Hospital*[5] the court held that a hospital was not vicariously liable for a doctor when carrying out his 'professional duties', because the employer had neither the knowledge nor the ability to exercise control over the doctor when he was carrying out those duties. Interestingly, in this case, the court also held that the nurses involved were acting under the control of the consultant and so the hospital was not vicariously liable for their negligent acts either. Thus for many years the main responsibility of the hospitals was limited to the duty to select adequate medical staff.

However, some years later in 1942 both these decisions were overruled in *Gold v Essex CC*[6]. In this case it was held that a hospital was vicariously liable for the negligent acts of a radiology technician who caused permanent disfigurement to the face of an infant plaintiff (represented here by AD Denning QC

---

4. *Evans v Liverpool Corporation* [1906] 1 KB 160.
5. *Hillyer v St Bartholomew's Hospital* [1909] 2 KB 820.
6. *Gold v Essex CC* [1942] 2 KB 293.

who was later to become Master of the Rolls) when treating her for warts. By analogy this principle was also applied to the acts of the hospital's nursing staff.

Doubts as to whether this principle also applied to consultant doctors employed by hospitals were finally resolved in *Cassidy v Minister of Health*[7] where a hospital was held vicariously liable for the negligence of a house surgeon which led to a severe deterioration in the plaintiff's condition of Dupuytren's contracture. In this case Denning LJ (as he then was) traced the judicial reluctance to impose liability on hospital authorities, and explained that it arose partly as an attempt to prevent charities being burdened with liabilities they could ill-afford. He then went on to explain why it was necessary for a modern hospital to be vicariously liable for the negligent acts of all its staff:

> When hospital authorities undertake to treat a patient and themselves select, appoint and employ the professional men and women who are to give the treatment, they are responsible for the negligence of those persons in failing to give proper treatment, no matter whether they are doctors, surgeons, nurses or anyone else. Once hospital authorities are held responsible for nurses and radiographers, as they have been in *Gold*'s case, I can see no possible reason why they should not also be responsible for house surgeons and resident medical officers on their permanent staff ... where the doctor or surgeon, be he consultant or not, is employed and paid ... by the hospital authorities, I am of the opinion that the hospital authorities are liable for his negligence in treating the patient.

There were still doubts as to whether this principle applied to part-time staff. However, in *Roe v Minister of Health*[8], which concerned consolidated actions by two plaintiffs who had become quadriplegic following injection with contaminated ampoules of spinal anaesthetic, the matter appeared to be resolved. Although in this case it was found, as a matter of fact, that there had been no negligence on the part of the anaesthetist, the court held that in principle the minister could be vicariously liable for the negligent acts of a part time member of the hospital's medical staff.

Historically, nurses were considered to be independent contractors and hospitals were not automatically liable for their torts. However, following the decision in *Gold v Essex CC* it became clear that employing hospitals are both vicariously liable for the torts of their nursing staff, and may also be under a direct and non-delegable duty of care (not dependent on vicarious liability) to provide adequate nursing services and competent nursing staff to the patient (see p 156 below).

Where nurses are employed by an agency which then supplies their services to a hospital, or to an individual, the situation is less clear, although much will depend on the terms of the nurse's contract with the agency, the representation made by the agency to the hospital or individual, and the steps taken by the

---

7. *Cassidy v Minister of Health* [1951] 1 All ER 574.
8. *Roe v Minister of Health* [1954] 2 QB 66.

agency to provide a competent nurse. However, the supplying agency is unlikely to be liable for the torts of a nurse committed during the course of her work. In *Hall and Wife v Lees and others*[9] the Oldham Nursing Association which provided nursing staff for the local hospital was held not to be vicariously liable for the negligent acts of nurses provided by them, since the nurses were not employees of the association. If a nurse provided by an agency is working within a NHS managed unit or trust, it is probable that the hospital would be vicariously liable for the nurses' tortious acts because of the degree of control exercised by the hospital over her acts which would render her either an employee or agent of the hospital. Alternatively, the hospital might be held to be in breach of its primary non-delegable duty (see below) to provide competent staff, and thus liable for the acts of nursing staff, regardless of the identity of the employer.

The personal, non-delegable duty of care owed by health authorities and hospitals

Quite separate from the vicarious liability owed by the health authority or NHS trust for the negligent acts of employees, there would appear to be an additional duty of care owed by the employer to its patients. This is described as a direct, non-delegable duty of care owed by the hospital or health authority, which is personal and not dependent on the doctrine of vicarious liability. One well-understood aspect of this is the employer's duty is to employ competent staff, to provide reasonable facilities within the hospital and to exercise of a reasonable level of supervision over staff (cf *Wilsons & Clyde Co v English*[10] in a non-medical context).

Thus, where for technical legal reasons, a plaintiff is unable to show that it was the *negligence* of an employee of a hospital acting in the course of his employment that has caused his injury, he may still have a cause of action directly against the hospital on the grounds, for instance, that it failed to provide doctors of sufficient skill and experience, or that the organisation of the hospital was in some way inadequate. Thus in *Wilsher v Essex AHA*[11] Mustill LJ suggested that such liability existed where a junior doctor who wrongly inserted an oxygen monitoring catheter into a baby's vein instead of into its artery, and was unable to comprehend the significance of the misleading and dangerous results provided. In this case Browne Wilkinson V-C (with whom Glidewell LJ agreed) stated:

> In my judgment a health authority which so conducts its hospital that it fails to provide doc-

---

9. *Hall and Wife v Lees and others* [1904] 2 KB 602.
10. *Wilsons & Clyde Co v English* [1938] AC 57.
11. *Wilsher v Essex Area Health Authority* [1987] 2 WLR 425 at 437.

tors of sufficient skill and experience to give the treatment offered at the hospital may be directly liable in negligence to the patient.

Similarly, in *Bull v Devon AHA*[12] the plaintiff, who claimed that her son had been born disabled due to asphyxia at birth, alleged that this asphyxia was due to the fact that the delivery of her son was delayed because a doctor was not available to attend her labour. This, she alleged was due to the fact that the hospital was organised in such a way as to function on two separate sites, and the system for summoning doctors from one site to another had broken down. Dillon LJ held that:

... the plaintiff has succeeded in proving, by ordinary civil standards of proof, that the failure to provide Mrs Bull with the prompt attendance that she needed was attributable to the negligence of the defendants in implementing an unreliable and essentially unsatisfactory system, for calling the registrar.

A second, and perhaps more contentious aspect of this personal non-delegable duty is the suggestion that a hospital, or NHS trust, owes a separate duty to ensure that due care is taken in the provision of medical treatment for patient. In *Cassidy*, Denning LJ explained this duty in the following way:

If a man goes to a doctor because he is ill, no one doubts that the doctor must exercise reasonable care and skill in his treatment of him and that is so whether the doctor is paid for his services or not. But if the doctor is unable to treat the man himself, and sends him to hospital, *are not the hospital authorities then under a duty of care in their treatment of him? I think they are.* (Emphasis added.)

In the past this second type of primary liability was unlikely to have been of importance to a plaintiff, given that in most cases the negligent actor is an employee of the health authority for whose acts it will be vicariously liable. Even today, where one NHS trust hospital 'lends' a doctor to another, the doctrine of vicarious liability as defined in *Mersey Docks & Harbour Board v Coggins & Griffiths*[13] would probably apply, ie the 'general' employer would remain vicariously liable for his negligent acts. If this second type of personal non-delegable liability does exist however, then the second NHS trust hospital who 'borrows' the consultant, will also be liable for failing to ensure proper treatment.

However, where a patient is treated in a private hospital or clinic, the doctor treating the patient will be an independent contractor, using the facilities of the hospital for a fee. Here the only possible form of liability which the hospital might owe for failing to ensure the proper treatment of such a patient would lie under this second type of primary liability. Thus a patient could argue that a hospital which held itself out as providing a reasonable standard of care in the treatment of particular types of illness, failed to ensure his non negligent treat-

---

12. *Bull v Devon AHA* [1993] 4 Med LR 117.
13. *Mersey Docks & Harbour Board v Coggins & Griffiths* [1947] AC 1.

ment by entering into a contractual relationship with a doctor who was not sufficiently competent to provide that form of treatment.

Liability of the Secretary of State

There has, from time to time, been litigation against the Secretary of State for Health on the grounds that the holder of that post may also owe a common law duty of care to individual patients.

The issue was considered in the *HIV Haemophiliac Litigation* case[14] where the plaintiffs were haemophiliacs (or their wives and/or children) who had developed AIDS as a result of being treated with contaminated blood imported from the US. They claimed that the Department of Health had been negligent in failing to ensure that England was self sufficient in providing its own blood products and that this negligence had caused the import of blood products from the US which in turn had caused their present condition.

The case was initially argued on the basis that the Department of Health did not owe a duty of care to the plaintiffs, however both Ralph Gibson and Bingham LJJ agreed that in principle a duty of care *was* owed to the plaintiffs by the government department; however, the plaintiffs would then have to show that the Department of Health was in breach of this duty by failing to allocate adequate funds to ensure that the country was self-sufficient in the provision of blood products. At this stage the distinction between the formulation of national health policy and its subsequent operational implementation gave rise to difficulties for the plaintiffs who eventually received an ex gratia payment from the government who did not admit liability.

It was also argued in the *Haemophiliacs'* case that the Secretary of State (or delegate) may be liable for breach of statutory duty as well as in negligence.

The National Health Service Act 1977, s 3(1) provides that:

It is the Secretary of State's duty to provide throughout England and Wales, to such extent as he considers necessary to meet all reasonable requirements –

(a)   hospital accommodation;

(b)   other accommodation for the purpose of any service provided under this Act;

(c)   medical, dental, nursing and ambulance services;

(d)   such other facilities for the care of expectant and nursing mothers and young children as he considers are appropriate as part of the health service;

---

14. *HIV Haemophiliac Litigation* case [1990] NLJR 1349.

(e)   such facilities for the prevention of illness, the care of persons suffering from illness and the after care of persons who have suffered from illness as he considers are appropriate;

(f)   such other services as are required for the treatment and diagnosis of illness.

These duties are, in turn, delegated to health authorities and the Act makes it plain that it is they, rather than the Secretary of State, who will be liable in the event that they fail to carry out their statutory duties (Sched 5, Part 15(1) to the Act) refers. The question of whether a cause of action for breach of statutory duty lies against the minister was considered in the *HIV Litigation* case. Here Ralph Gibson LJ following the unreported decision of Wien J in *R v Secretary of State for Social Services and others ex p Hincks*[15] held that the 1977 Act did not demonstrate the intention of Parliament to impose a duty which could be enforced by civil action.

Resource issues

There are many cases where the provision of health care depends on the level of resources made available for treatment. In most cases the funds allocated to health authorities by the Secretary State are then re-allocated by the relevant health authority on the basis of perceived need. The question then arises: to what extent should the courts be used as a mechanism by aggrieved patients to force the relevant health authorities to provide them with the treatment they need. This matter was first addressed in *Wilsher v Essex Area Health Authority*[16] by Browne-Wilkinson V-C where he stated:

> Given limited resources, what balance is to be struck in the allocation of such resources between compensating those whose treatment is not wholly successful, and the provision of required treatment for the world at large. But I do not think the courts will do society a favour by distorting the existing law so as to conceal the real social questions that arise.

In *R v Secretary of State for Social Services and others ex p Hincks*[17], four orthopaedic patients sought a declaration that the Secretary of State was in breach of the duties imposed on him under the National Health Service Act 1977, s 1 to provide a comprehensive health service because they had been obliged to wait for periods longer than was medically desirable for their operations.

In his judgment Lord Denning MR described the main lines of argument on behalf of the plaintiffs as follows.

> Mr Blom Cooper ... has referred us to the fact that there are no provisions in the statute

---

15. *R v Secretary of State for Social Services and others ex p Hincks* [1980] 1 BMLR 93.

16. *Wilsher v Essex Area Health Authority* [1986] 3 All ER 801.

17. See n 15

which limit the expenditure of the department. Section 3(1) of the National Health Service Act 1977 provides (for the duty of the Minister of Health in respect of NHS provision, see above) ... He says that that duty must be fulfilled. If the Secretary of State needs money to do it then he must see that Parliament gives it him. Alternatively if Parliament does not give it him then a provision should be put in the statute to excuse him from the duty. Mr Blom Cooper says that the duty is plain and imperative and it ought to be fulfilled by the Secretary of State.

However Lord Denning's response to this line of argument was to hold that the issue of the allocation of health care and resources was 'non justiciable' (ie not a matter for the courts). He quoted with approval from the judgment of Wien J at first instance who said:

If funds were unlimited then of course regions and areas could go ahead and provide all sorts of services. But funds are not unlimited. The funds are voted by Parliament, and the health service has to do the best it can with the total allocation of health resources.

Lord Denning concluded his judgment by saying that:

The Secretary of State says that he is doing the best he can with the limited resources available to him: and I do not think he can be faulted in that matter.

Thus the courts cannot interfere with the Secretary of State for Health's duties under the 1977 Act unless it can be shown that the minister had acted in a manner which was held by the court to be unreasonable (see *Associated Provincial Picture Houses v Wednesbury Corporation*[18]).

Similar decisions were also taken in *R v Central Birmingham HA ex p Walker*[19] and *R v Central Birmingham HA ex p Collier*[20]. Here, both infant plaintiffs, who required urgent hole in the heart by-pass surgery, were refused leave for judicial review of the health authority's failure to allocate sufficient resources for their operations. In both cases the courts held that they had no power to allocate financial resources within the health authority. In *Ex p Walker*, which concerned a baby where surgery had been postponed five times because of a shortage of skilled nursing staff Sir, John Donaldson MR stated that:

It is not for this court, or indeed any court to substitute its own judgment for the judgment of those who are responsible for the allocation of resources. This court could only intervene when it was satisfied that there was a *prima facie* case, not only of failing to allocate resources in the way in which others think they should be allocated, but of failure to allocate resources to an extent that was Wednesbury unreasonable.

He went on to point out that, were the courts to encourage patients to go to law on every occasion that they did not receive the health care to which they believed they were entitled, this in itself would be an expense to the relevant

18. *Associated Provincial Picture Houses v Wednesbury Corporation* [1947] 2 All ER 680.
19. *R v Central Birmingham HA ex p Walker* [1987] 3 BMLR 32.
20. *R v Central Birmingham HA ex p Collier* (1988) LEXIS 6 January.

health authority who might otherwise have spent those funds on the treatment of patients.

In *Ex p Collier*, where the condition of the child concerned was even more urgently in need of treatment than in *Walker*, Stephen Browne LJ said:

> In the absence of any evidence which could begin to show that there was [such a failure] to allocate resources in this instance ... there can be no arguable case ... It does seem to me to be unfortunate that this procedure has been adopted. It is wholly misconceived in my view. The courts of this country cannot arrange the lists in the hospital ... and should not be asked to intervene.

The basic principle underlying these decisions is that the courts will not make orders which they cannot supervise, and that in the context of medical treatment the final decision must be taken by medical, not legal, experts. In *Re J (a minor)*[21] J a 16 month old child was profoundly handicapped as a result of hitting his head in an accidental fall when he was one month old. He was microcephalic and suffered from a severe form of cerebral palsy, cortical blindness and epilepsy. His expectation of life was uncertain, but undoubtedly short. The consultant pediatrician in charge of the infant was of the opinion that it would not be medically appropriate to intervene with intensive therapeutic measures such as artificial ventilation if J were to suffer a life threatening event and that although it would be appropriate to offer J suction treatment, physiotherapy and antibiotic treatment, it would not be appropriate to subject him to more intensive measures if he became unable to breathe spontaneously.

The local authority, which had placed the child with foster parents, sought and was granted leave under the Children Act 1989, s 100 to invoke the inherent jurisdiction of the High Court to determine whether artificial ventilation and other life saving measures should be provided if he suffered a life-threatening event, and sought an order requiring the health authority to continue to provide J with all available treatment, including intensive resuscitation.

In line with the earlier cases, the court held that it was 'absolutely undesirable' that it should make an order which would have the effect of compelling a health authority to make available 'scarce resources to a particular child without knowing whether or not there were other patients to whom those resources might more advantageously be devoted'.

It is instructive to note that following these judgments there was no action in negligence against the North West Thames Health Authority where a unit which treated children with a rare metabolic disorder had been closed (*R v NW Thames HA ex p Daniels*[22]) although the health authority was criticised by the court for its administrative failures.

---

21. *Re J (a minor) (wardship: medical treatment)* [1993] Fam 15.
22. *R v NW Thames HA ex p Daniels* [1993] 4 Med LR 364.

The most recent in this line of decisions, in the widely publicised case of *B v Cambridge Area Health Authority*[23]. In this case B, a 10 year old girl was suffering from acute myeloid leukemia; following earlier chemotherapy, irradiation and a bone marrow transplant, B suffered a relapse. Further courses of chemotherapy and a second bone marrow transplant were proposed, however the court was told that her chances of surviving this treatment were low, being estimated at between 10 per cent and 20 per cent. However, without such treatment it was agreed that she would survive for only another six to eight weeks.

The respondent health authority, which estimated the costs of the proposed treatment as being about £75,000, decided not to provide the treatment, the decision being taken on two grounds. The first ground for the decision was a clinical one: it would not be in the child's best interests to provide such treatment since the possibility of its success was low and the effects of the treatment unpleasant. The second ground for the decision related to the high cost of the treatment and the fact that the health authority's resources were not unlimited. In the High Court, Laws J said that the question for the court to decide was whether the respondents had taken a decision which interfered with the applicant's right to life, and, if they had, whether they had offered a substantial public interest justification for doing so. He concluded that it was in the best interests of the child that she should receive the treatment and that the public interest was not sufficiently substantial to warrant the health authority's refusal. The action of the authority in denying treatment had not been reasonable and he quashed the decision on that basis.

On appeal the same day, the decision of the High Court was overturned. The Court of Appeal declined to interfere with the decision of the health authority on the grounds that the authority had not exceeded its powers or acted unreasonably in the legal sense of the word, and that the powers of the court were not such that it could substitute its own decision for that of the authority making it. Sir Thomas Bingham MR stated:

> While I have every possible sympathy with B, I feel bound to regard this as an attempt – wholly understandable but nevertheless misguided – to involve the court in a field of activity where it is not fitted to make any decision favourable to the patient.

He went on to say that in a perfect world no doubt any treatment sought would be provided no matter how much it would cost, if a life were potentially at stake, but that the court could not proceed the basis that we lived in such a world. It was common knowledge, he said, that health authorities were pressed for funds and that difficult and agonising decisions had to be made as to how a limited budget could best be allocated for the maximum number of patients.

Sir Louis Blom Cooper QC commenting on the decision suggested that there was a clear need for an ethics committee to be set up:

23. *B v Cambridge Area Health Authority* (1995) *The Times* 11 March.

Decisions about who gets treatment must be for the health authority. Right to life means the right to protection from any outside interference, not the right to demand treatment.

Ironically the health authority's costs for the court action (approximately £15,000) and the similar level of the plaintiffs costs (which were met by legal aid funds) would no doubt have gone some way to providing the child with the treatment sought, which was subsequently provided privately by a charitable donor.

Crown indemnity

Until 1 January 1990, where a doctor was found to be personally liable in negligence, or where a health authority was found to be vicariously or personally liable, the cost of compensating the plaintiff fell directly on the defendants.

Doctors were required as a part of their contracts of employment with health authorities to purchase insurance with the Medical Defence Union or the Medical Protection Society; these bodies provided legal advice and representation for doctors and indemnified them against any award of damages made against them. Two-thirds of the cost of insurance for hospital doctors was born by the health authorities and the full cost of insurance for GPs was paid by the FHSA (formerly FPC). Where compensation was awarded against a doctor and a health authority, the normal practice was for the health authority and the defence association to agree to split the cost 50:50 (1954 (HM(54)32)) without recourse to litigation, unless it could be shown that one party was entirely to blame.

Unfortunately during the 1980s the rate and cost of litigation in medical negligence cases increased, as did the cost of doctors' insurance. The Medical Protection Society began to charge differential rates which reflected the risks of practising in the different specialities (eg obstetrics and gynaecology was a more risky and thus expensive speciality to insure that geriatrics).

Doctors and health authorities became increasingly concerned at the cost of membership of the defence societies which both shared, and health authorities were concerned that the expensive conduct of litigation was entirely in the hands of the defence organisations. Thus, pressure was brought to bear on the government to abandon the system of insurance in favour of an NHS indemnity scheme, whereby health authorities would assume direct financial responsibility for all claims brought against doctors in their employment. This scheme was eventually introduced on 1 January 1990 by means of circular HC(89)34 ('Claims of Medical negligence Against NHS Hospitals and Community Doctors and Dentists').

For claims lodged after 1 January 1990 health authorities (and, since 1 April 1991, NHS trusts), which as corporate bodies are legally liable for the negligent acts of their employees, will be formally responsible for the handling and financing of claims in negligence against medical and dental staff. Each health authority or trust will decide how it wishes claims to be handled and they may, if they so wish, make use of the services of the medical defence organisations at an agreed rate, although they may also, if they so wish use in-house or other legal advisers. In deciding how a case should be handled health authorities are particularly advised to pay attention to any view expressed by the doctors concerned and to any potentially damaging effect on the reputation of the practitioner. They should also have regard to any point of principle raised by the case, an the costs involved in defending it.

Up until 1 April 1991 health authorities would be required to meet any claim up to a maximum figure of £80,000, the remainder being met from the accrued resources of the medical defence organisations. After that date NHS managed units and NHS trusts will pay any awards of damages against them up to a specified amount (0.5 per cent of the annual budget at the time of writing); the remainder is met from government loans *which must be repaid over a period of 10 years* at an agreed rate of interest. No additional funding is made available to the health authorities to meet these claims, and while this may have the effect of encouraging them to develop risk management strategies to reduce claims against them, it may also have the effect of limiting the health care provision available to patients within the area.

The scheme does not extend to general practitioners who must still be insured with one of the medical defence organisations.

CASE STUDY ONE

Dr Ross was an honourary medical officer at the private wing of an NHS Trust Hospital. He received no payment for services performed at the hospital but was allowed to use the hospital's operating theatre for his own patients on a roster basis. In consideration of this right, Dr Ross was required to be on call for emergency admissions to the hospital at certain times without payment.

Is the hospital liable for any negligent mistakes Dr Ross might make in treating any patient in the hospital (whether private patient or otherwise?).

CASE STUDY TWO

Jennifer Smith, aged six years, attended her local primary school where she received specialist tuition. She was born with a heart defect and required resuscitation at birth. Although her parents were informed that she would need cardiac surgery when she was older, they did not suspect that she would be in any way handicapped, nor were they advised as to such a possibility. By the age of two years it became apparent that Jennifer was not progressing normally; her physical development was retarded in comparison with other children. It was also discovered that her hearing was poor.

Within a year of commencing school Jennifer's condition began to deteriorate further. She could not take part in any physical activities, constantly suffered from infections and become withdrawn and agitated. The school is extremely concerned about her condition.

The parents, in November 1994, put pressure on the GP and the school health service to intervene with the hospital (an NHS trust) to force it to admit Jennifer with a view to undertaking the necessary surgery. The school nurse, Mrs Brown, who had become very involved with the family and had spent a good deal of time talking over with them the implications of Jennifer's condition was told, on enquiry to the hospital, that there were other more urgent cases and the necessary resources were not available in the financial year ending March 1995.

In January 1995 Jennifer's parents separated because of the strain of caring for a handicapped child. At the beginning of April 1995 the hospital admitted Jennifer to the children's ward. Jennifer's mother is informed that the only chance of Jennifer's survival was for her to undergo transplant surgery at a specialist hospital. Jennifer's father, who has seen her on only two occasions since he separated from her mother, refused to give consent to such an operation in the event of a donor being found.

Jennifer's mother begged Mrs Brown to contact her husband and persuade him to give consent otherwise she fears that the hospital will refuse to undertake the transplant.

Advise Mrs Brown on the following:

- whether Mr and Mrs Smith could have forced the hospital to treat Jennifer at an earlier stage and whether their refusal to do so was unlawful;

- if, in the event that it could not be proved that earlier surgical intervention would have obviated the necessity for Jennifer to undergo transplant surgery, Mrs Smith could bring an action against the hospital on Jennifer's behalf, for compensation.

- whether the hospital would need to have Mr Smith's consent before they undertook transplant surgery.

13   Law and the Elderly

Age structure of the population

The total population of the UK is currently nearly 58 million, of whom 9.1 million are aged over 65. Of this group 2.2 million are aged over 80. By the year 2031 it is projected that the total number of people aged over 80 will be 3.4 million and by that year it is also projected that the number of deaths per annum will be more than the number of births.

The incidence of some form of dementing illness clearly increases with advancing age. It is estimated that 1:10 of people aged over 65 suffer from dementia, and in the 80+ age group the incidence is 1:5. As yet, there is no cure for such illnesses, although research in this area is beginning to show promising developments.

While the community care policies of the present government are aimed at maintaining people in the community for as long as possible the cost to the health service of the elderly is extremely high (health service expenditure on those aged 75 and over is estimated at £1,300 per person per annum).

The cost of residential care for the elderly is similarly high and increasing. Over the last 10 years we have seen a significant shift from public to private residential care and the estimated cost per week of such care is as follows:

- residential care for the elderly not requiring specialist nursing care can range from £200-500+ per week;

- residential nursing care for the elderly will cost anything between £350-800+ per week depending on the facilities provided.

The cost of domiciliary care in the home is equally expensive. The British Nursing Association's current costs for private domiciliary nursing care are approximately £15-20 per hour (unqualified care staff would be somewhat cheaper).

Government statistics indicate that less than 4 per cent of the elderly population are currently in residential care. It is projected, however, that by the end of the century there will be nearly one million people aged 85 in the population of whom 20 per cent will be in residential care. This is despite the recent emphasis on the development and expansion of 'community care' services in the National Health Service and Community Care Act 1990.

Community care

The National Health Service and Community Care Act is based on the White Paper 'Caring for People'[1] in which six key objectives were listed:

- to promote the development of domiciliary, day and respite services to enable people to live in their own homes wherever feasible and sensible;

- to ensure that service providers make practical support for carers a high priority;

- to make proper assessments of need and good case management the cornerstone of high quality care;

- to promote the development of a flourishing independent sector alongside good quality public services;

- to clarify the responsibilities of agencies and so make it easier to hold them to account for their performance;

- to secure better value for tax-payer's money by introducing a new funding structure for social care[2].

As has become evident recently there are serious problems, at least in some local authority areas[3], about funding community care provision adequately. It is clearly not a cheaper alternative to residential care and indeed could be considerably more expensive for very disabled (or demented) people.

The National Health Service and Community Care Act, s 47(1) places a duty on local authority social services departments to undertake an assessment of a person's needs for community care services 'where it appears to a local authority that any person for whom they may provide or arrange for the provision of community care may be in need of any such services'. The duty under the Act is, however, limited. There is neither a right to demand an assessment, nor is there an obligation placed on the local authority to make provision for any identified need. Department of Health policy guidance[4] states that 'assessment should take account of the wishes of the individual and his or her carer' and that 'they should feel that the process is aimed at meeting their wishes'.

---

1. Department of Health [1989].
2. See, eg the National Assistance Act 1948, Part III and the Mental Health Act 1983, s 117.
3. See, eg Lancashire County Council's decision to withdraw 24-hour home care from a resident on the grounds that residential care would be a cheaper option, reported by the Press Association, 'Pensioner's Legal Fight for Community Care' 28 February 1995.
4. Department of Health (1989d) and (1990).

Where, however, a person (aged 18 or over) is disabled or suffering from serious ill health (which includes mental disorder)[5] there is a statutory obligation[6] on the local authority to make certain specified provisions available to meet the needs of that person. These include the following: social work support, rehabilitation centres, hostel accommodation, free or subsidised travel, warden assisted housing, practical help in the home, holidays, meals on wheels, help with telephone, television, library facilities etc. Local authorities are also under an obligation to compile and maintain a register of every disabled person in their area (over the age of 18). Eligibility for assistance is independent of whether the person is registered or not[7].

Once need is established, the local authority's obligation is to meet that need within a reasonable period of time (irrespective of financial constraints). Local authorities have the right to charge for services (other than the cost of assessment or giving of information) if they wish to do so[8].

Promoting the welfare needs of the elderly

Under the Health Services and Public Health Act 1968 s 45(1):

> A local authority may, with the approval of the Secretary of State, and, to such extent as he may direct, make arrangements for promoting the welfare of old people.

The Secretary of State[9] has approved the development of the following; the provision of meals and recreational facilities in the home or elsewhere; the provision of information about relevant services; the provision of transport to help with travelling to and from local authority or similar services; the provision of social work support; the provision of practical assistance in the home, including adaptations; sheltered housing; and assistance in finding suitable boarding out placements for the elderly. These provisions are in addition to the duties under the Chronically Sick and Disabled Persons Act 1970 referred to above and thus do not have to be provided unless the person falls within the definition of 'disables' within the National Assistance Act 1948, s 29.

Under s 45(3) the local authority can employ, as its agent, a voluntary organisation or other person whose activities include the provision of services to elderly people.

---

5. Defined in the National Assistance Act 1948, s 29(1).
6. Chronically Sick and Disabled Persons Act 1970, s 2(1).
7. Department of Health Circular LAC (93)(10).
8. See para 13.4.
9. DHSS Circular 19/71.

Helping the carer

While the Department of Health's policy guidance[10] to local authorities on their duties under the National Health Service and Community Care Act points out that carers' wishes should be taken into account when any assessment of need is undertaken, there has been considerable concern expressed by groups such as the Carers' National Association that this is not happening. There are an estimated 1.5 million full-time carers in this country who, according to the British Medical Association[11], save the state some £34 billion. The Carers' (Recognition and Services) Bill 1995, a private member's bill, received its second reading on 3 March 1995[12] and has the government's backing. The bill, if it becomes law, will give carers a right to an assessment of their own needs, and place on local authorities a duty to make provision, eg for respite care, to meet such needs. The Association of Social Services Directors have estimated that it will cost local authorities £40 million to fund the cost of assessments alone. The on-costs have not, as yet, been calculated.

Charging for community care

A local authority is entitled to make a 'reasonable' charge for any non-residential service[13]. 'Reasonableness' is determined by reference to two criteria[14], first the cost to the local authority of making the relevant provision, and second the means of the user: 'the local authority shall not require him to pay more for it than it appears to them that it is reasonably practicable for him to pay.'[15]. An increasing number of local authorities now charge for services in this area and the annual revenue support grant paid to local authorities annually is based on the assumption that charges are in fact made.

Complaints and legal remedies

Every local authority is required to have established a complaints procedure by 1 April 1991. Oral complaints should be resolved informally where possible. If this is not possible, then the complainant must be invited to make a written complaint, with an explanation of the procedure. Advice and help in drafting

---

10. Department of Health (1989d).
11. BMA.
12. See *The Guardian* 2 March 1995.
13. The National Assistance Act 1948, s 22 requires a local authority to charge for residential accommodation.
14. The Social Services Inspectorate (1994) has given advise on the operation of the 'reasonableness' tests within s 17.
15. Section 17(3).

the complaint must also be given or information on obtaining independent advice. On receipt of a written complaint the authority must make a formal, written response within 28 days (or the complainant be told in writing why such a response cannot be made within this time limit). If the complaint is still not resolved a review panel must be set up to consider it.

Unresolved complaints can be referred to the Parliamentary Commissioner for Local Administration (the ombudsman). Before the ombudsman can hear a complaint he 'shall satisfy himself that the complaint has been brought ... to the notice of the authority ... and that the authority has been afforded a reasonable opportunity to investigate, and to reply, to the complainant'[16].

In his investigations into complaints against local authorities[17] the ombudsman has made it clear that complainants must be made aware of their rights to challenge outcomes. The ombudsman's investigations and findings deal with how decisions are made, and whether the authority has complied with its statutory obligations rather than whether the decision is right or wrong.

If a complainant feels that a local authority has failed to comply with any of its statutory duties and the complaints procedures outlined above have been exhausted the complainant can ask the Secretary of State to intervene[18]. The Secretary of State has power to issue an order declaring the authority to be in default where he is satisfied that the authority has failed, without reasonable cause, to comply with its statutory duties.

An application for judicial review is available, with permission of the High Court, to a person who believes that a local authority's actions, procedures or decisions are so unreasonable that they would not have been taken by any reasonable authority[19], or they are *ultra vires* (exceed) or in breach of their powers. A pensioner, Mrs Emily Whalley, has recently been granted permission by the High Court to challenge the decision of Lancashire County Council to withdraw her 24-hour-a-day community care package on the grounds that it is too expensive and that she should accept a place in a residential home[20].

Residential and nursing care

Under Part III of the National Assistance Act 1948, a local authority has a duty to provide residential accommodation for 'persons who by reason of age, infirmity, or any other circumstances are in need of care and attention which is not

---

16. Local Government Act 1974, s 26(5).
17. See Report by the Local Government Ombudsman into Complaints No 90/A/2675.
18. Local Authority Social Services Act 1970, s 7(d).
19. *Associated Provincial Picture House v Wednesbury Corporation* [1947] 2 All ER 680.
20. 'Pensioner's Legal Fight for Community Care' (see n 3 above).

otherwise available to them'[21]. Such accommodation may be provided by the local authority, a voluntary organisation or private home registered under the Registered Homes Act 1984. Over half the beds are now in fact provided by the voluntary or private sector[22].

Compulsory admission

The Act provides for the compulsory admission to residential accommodation of people who are:

(a) suffering from grave chronic disease or, being aged, infirm or physically incapacitated, are living in insanitary conditions; and

(b) are unable to devote to themselves, and are not receiving from other persons, proper care and attention[23].

A local authority can only apply to the court for an order if it has first obtained a written certificate from a medical officer employed by the district health authority which can only be issued after 'thorough inquiry and consideration'.

Such detention does not allow for any form of treatment without the person's consent.

An order lasts for three months and can be extended, by the court, for a further three months. The detained person can apply to the court for revocation of the order after a period of six weeks has elapsed[24].

The local authority is entitled to charge for the accommodation provided. This is unlike the provisions under the Public Health Act 1961, s 36 which gives local authorities the power to require a person to move out of their home because it is deemed insanitary. Here accommodation must be provided free of charge[25].

In practice there are only approximately 200 such compulsory admissions per year but clearly the legislation raises important civil liberties issues. After all, a person might be quite happy to live in the way he is without state interference.

An elderly person suffering from mental disorder may also, of course, be subject to the compulsory provisions of the Mental Health Act.

---

21. Midwinter (1992).
22. National Assistance Act 1948, s (1)(a) and (b).
23. National Assistance Act 1948, s 49(1)(a) and (b).
24. National Assistance Act 1948, s 47(6).
25. See Law Commission Consultative Paper (1993c).

Payment of fees for residential and nursing home care

Prior to the introduction of the National Health Service and Community Care Act, responsibility for the payment of residential or nursing home fees of people who were unable to fund themselves vested in the Department of Social Security. Since 1 April 1993 this responsibility has now passed to local authority social services departments. To be successful the applicant must pass two tests:

- A needs test

If the SSD, after having undertaken an assessment in accordance with s 47 National Health Service and Community Care Act 1990, decides that the person does not need residential accommodation, help towards the fees will be unavailable. If, however, the elderly person is assessed as being in need of residential accommodation, the local authority has a duty to meet that need.

One area of growing concern is the responsibility for funding private nursing home care. Local authorities do not have a duty to provide accommodation for a person who is a hospital in-patient. Hospitals are increasingly discharging patients who continue to need nursing care, eg following surgery. Disputes can arise as to whether it is the district health authority or the local authority who is liable to pay any fees arising from this eventuality. The legislation is unclear. If a local authority is involved in the assessment of a person for nursing home care it seems that the local authority have a duty to pay (subject to the provisions of the means test set out below)[26]. All local and health authorities should have established a protocol which sets out a strategy for deciding on payment for nursing home beds and for assessments prior to hospital discharge.

- A means test

This involves the SSD making up the difference between a person's income and the amount of fees charged by the home, allowing the individual to keep a personal allowance (currently £13.10 per week). The changes to the benefit rules are contained in the Social Security Benefits (Amendments Consequential Upon the Introduction of Community Care) Regulations 1992. If the needs test has been satisfied a person entering such a home may claim the following (in addition to any state retirement pension, etc payable):

(a) income support (subject to the pre-existing means test) at the same rate as if he was living in the community including –

---

26. DoH Circular LAC(92)(24) para 3 of Annex.

(i) a residential allowance worth £45 per week (£50 in the Greater London Area);

(ii) social services department's contribution to make up any shortfall.

(Note that people in local authority residential accommodation cannot claim the £45 per week residential allowance which is available for residents in private homes. Although this does not affect individual residents it does increase the cost of accommodation for local authorities. This is thus an encouragement to local authorities to phase out their own residential home provision.)

Savings of under £3,000 are disregarded. Between £3,000 and £8,000 £1 per week is assumed for each £250. If capital exceeds £8,000 full contribution is required until the person assets fall below this sum.

Social services departments do not necessarily have to meet the full cost of the fees. They need only pay what they regard as reasonable for that type of accommodation. Thus the resident/family may still be obliged to make up any shortfall even though they fall within the income support limits.

Individuals entering a residential home who receive attendance allowance or the care component of the disabled living allowance will continue to receive this for the first four weeks of their stay (but it will be regarded for assessment purposes as part of their income). At the end of the four weeks the payments will stop and will be replaced by income support. For those people who are funding their own fees for residential/nursing home accommodation attendance allowance or disabled living allowance is still claimable.

Choice of home

The Department of Health memorandum (Financing of community care arrangements after April 1993 and of individual choice of accommodation, 2 October 1992) states that a local authority must place a person in his/her 'preferred accommodation' provided that:

• suitability is determined by the local authority;

• the cost is no more than is usually paid for a person with those needs (unless a third party (other than a spouse) can be found to make up the difference); and

• the accommodation is available and is in the UK.

In R v Avon County Council ex p Hazell[27] the court quashed the decision of the local authority which had refused to allow Mr Hazell to go to a home of his choice. Avon's ground for refusal was that the fees were too high. The court,

---

27. *R v Avon County Council ex p Hazell* [1993] QBD, 5 July, Ref CO/659/92.

however, held that, as other residents were being funded there by the same local authority, their refusal to fund Mr Hazell was unlawful. In two cases involving the closure of homes and the re-location of the residents to other accommodation[28] the Court of Appeal held that consultation with residents had to be made well in advance of closure and residents' objections should be considered.

Payment of fees

Local authorities are required to charge residents for accommodation at the 'standard rate fixed for that accommodation'[29]. Little discretion exists as to how any assessment of a person's ability to pay is made[30].

Capital and the owner occupier

If a person enters a residential home for a temporary stay the value of his residential property is disregarded for assessment purposes. The Supplementary Benefits Act 1976, Sched 1, para 17 states clearly that only a dwelling which is not the person's residence can be included for assessment purposes. Thus the important issue is in determining at what point in time a person in residential care is deemed to have given up his ('former') home.

For a person entering long stay care the property owned and lived in by them alone will be counted as capital. As the value of the property will exceed £8,000 that person will be fully liable for the fees (see below). Local authorities are not, however, under any statutory obligation to take the dwelling house into account for assessment purposes and it is suggested that a local authority that operates a rigid policy in this respect might be deemed to be fettering its discretion and thereby acting *ultra vires* (*Attorney General ex rel Tilley v London Borough of Wandsworth*)[31].

If someone else lives in the property (in whole or in part) its value will be disregarded if the person is either a spouse or partner or a 'relative' aged over 60 or 'incapacitated'. The term 'relative' includes parent, son, son-in-law, daughter, daughter-in-law, brother, sister (plus spouse or partner of any of the above), grandparent, grandchild, uncle, aunt, nephew, niece). The term 'incapacitated' is not formally defined, but it would include any person in receipt of an attendance allowance, etc.

---

28. *R v Devon County Council ex p Baker* and *R v Durham County Council ex p Broxson and Curtis* (1993) *The Times* 21 January.

29. National Assistance Act 1948, s 22.

30. Charging for Residential Accommodation Guide issued under the Local Authority Social Services Act 1970, s 7(1).

31. *Attorney General ex rel Tilley v London Borough of Wandsworth* [1981] 1 All ER 1162.

The local authority has the discretion to ignore the value of the property if a person is living in it but does not fall into the above categories. The same rules concerning the exercise by the local authority of its discretionary powers as indicated above will apply.

Charges on property

The local authority has no power under the legislation to force the sale of the property to allow for collection of the fees. If a person who has entered residential care (a resident) refuses to sell the local authority should undertake a professional estimate of the property's current selling price, less 10 per cent in recognition of the expenses which would be incurred were the property to be sold, and minus any mortgage or loan secured against the property[32]. Should the resident be unable to meet the assessment from available funds, the authority must agree a lower rate and defer levying the assessed amount, plus interest, until such time as the house is eventually sold. In the meantime, however, the local authority will probably wish to create a 'legal charge' over it.

Under s 22 Health and Social Services and Social Security Adjudications Act 1983[33] local authorities are empowered to create charges whenever residents have an interest in land and have failed to pay the assessed charge for accommodation. A legal charge over the property has the effect of preventing transfer of ownership (including sale) of the property without the knowledge of the holder of the charge. It will thus give that person the right to claim from the sale of the property any money owed (as a mortgagee of the property).

Liability of a spouse for fees

There is no power under the National Assistance Act 1948 to assess a couple according to their joint resources (unlike under the social security rules). However, the National Assistance Act 1948, s 42 places on spouses a duty to maintain the other. Thus a local authority can clearly look to a spouse for payment and in the event of refusal to pay may bring an action under the National Assistance Act 1948, s 48. In these circumstances the magistrates' court would decide whether a spouse should reasonably be expected to contribute and, if so, the amount.

Under Department of Social Security guidelines no contribution can be ordered if the spouse's resources become 'inadequate'.

---

32. DHAA (1978) para 19.
33. This section was brought into force on 12 April 1993 by SI 1992/2974.

Disposal of assets prior to entering residential care

Under s 21 Health and Social Services and Social Security Adjudications Act 1983 (brought into force on 12 April 1993 by SI 1992/2974) where a person who 'knowingly and with the intention of avoiding charges for the accommodation' has transferred assets to another person(s) within six months of entering residential care for less than its true value (or for no consideration at all) the local authority may recover the assets from the transferee(s).

Proving intent will be extremely difficult for a local authority and valuing the assets could also be problematic (eg if the local authority is denied access to undertake a valuation).

The procedure for complaints in respect of local authority provision and the legal remedies have been dealt with above. Complaints in respect of residents living in homes in the independent sector may be less effective. Where a 'home' is providing both accommodation and personal care the home must be registered with the local authority[34]. Homes providing nursing care must be registered with the district health authority. Registering authorities are required to make periodic inspections and all such homes are required to have a complaints procedure available to residents and their relatives or friends which provides for the name and address of the registering authority to whom complaints can be made[35]. The registering authority is under an obligation to investigate any complaints and has power under the Act to withdraw registration if a complaint, after appropriate investigation, is found to be sufficiently serious. It is a criminal offence to provide residential or nursing care accommodation without being registered[36].

Enduring powers of attorney and the Court of Protection

Physical or mental incapacity may prevent a person from being able to look after his own personal affairs. This problem clearly increases with advancing years. English law provides procedures which allow other people to assume responsibilities in respect of another person's property. Two important legal procedures, which are designed to protect the interests of the incapable person, are the grant of a power of attorney and application to the Court of Protection for appointment of a receiver.

---

34. Registered Homes Act 1984, s 1.
35. Registered Homes Act 1984, Sched 2.
36. Registered Homes Act 1984, s 2.

Mental incapacity

The law assumes that every person is competent to handle his own affairs unless the contrary is proved. A person can be deemed to be incapable of managing his own affairs whether or not he is detained under the Mental Health Act 1983 and whether or not he lives in his own home[37]. Mental incapacity means '... in relation to any person, that he is incapable by reason of mental disorder of managing his property and affairs'[38].

Power of attorney

If a person is mentally capable, but, because of physical incapacity is unable practically to deal with his own affairs although still capable of making decisions in respect of protecting that property, the legal position is straightforward. The common law allows that person to appoint another person to act on his behalf. A power of attorney is 'the authority given by one person to another to act for him in his absence, eg to convey land, receive debts, sue, etc'[39]. The person who executes a power of attorney is called the 'donor' of the power, the person who is appointed to act is called the attorney ('donee' of the power). If the attorney acts in breach of his powers he will be personally liable. He will thus be liable for any losses which are incurred as a result of acting outside the powers granted to him and may be criminally liable if there was an intention on his part to permanently deprive the donor of his property[40].

At common law, mental incapacity immediately revoked a power of attorney, although the Powers of Attorney Act 1971, s 5(1) does provide legal protection for attorneys who act in ignorance of that incapacity.

Enduring powers of attorney

It is now possible to grant a power of attorney which continues in force despite incapacity[41]. The Enduring Powers of Attorney Act 1985 allows a person with sufficient mental capacity to execute a power of attorney which will not take effect until the onset of mental incapacity. The Act provides three basic safeguards.

First, the enduring power of attorney must be granted on a prescribed form which contains an explanation of its consequences[42].

---

37. Mental Health Act 1983, s 93.
38. Enduring Powers of Attorney Act 1985, s 13.
39. Moseley and Whiteley's Law Dictionary London: Butterworths.
40. Theft Act 1968, s 4.
41. Enduring Powers of Attorney Act 1985.
42. Section 2(1).

The capacity necessary to grant the enduring power is that the donor understands 'in broad terms' the nature and effect of the enduring power of attorney. The donor does not have to be capable of managing all her property and affairs at the time. He need only understand that the attorney can assume control over all his affairs, can do anything he can do, can continue in power even if the donor becomes incapable, and that the power cannot be revoked without the confirmation of the Court of Protection in the event of his becoming mentally incapable[43]. If the donor wishes, the attorney may act while he is still mentally capable.

Second, once the donee of the power 'has reason to believe' that the donor is, or is becoming, mentally incapable of managing her property and affairs the attorney must apply to register the enduring power of attorney with the Court of Protection[44] and notify both the donor and his close relatives[45]. In practice it can be registered on the day it is made.

Relatives may object in the following circumstances:

- where the power is invalid;

- where the donor is not yet incapable;

- where the power was obtained by fraud or undue pressure;

- where the attorney is unsuitable[46].

Where there has been a failure to register, the power is automatically revoked.

Third, the Court of Protection has various supervisory functions once registration has taken place. It can cancel an enduring power of attorney in the following circumstances:

- where the donor remains capable;

- where the enduring power of attorney has been revoked or has expired;

- where the enduring power of attorney is invalid or has been obtained by fraud or undue pressure;

- where the attorney disclaims or is unsuitable without the confirmation of the Court of Protection;

- where the court itself assumes control over the donor's property and affairs.

---

43. *Re K* [1988] Ch 310.
44. Section 4(1).
45. Section 4(3) and Sched 1.
46. Section 6(4).

Additionally the Court of Protection has the following powers:

- to give directions to the attorney;

- to require accounts and information from him;

- to authorise him to do things which otherwise would need the donor's authority to do[47].

The court has no power to direct an attorney as to how to dispose of the donor's property, an enduring power of attorney's only legal responsibility is to ensure that the donor's finances and property are managed properly[48]. An enduring power of attorney cannot be used to authorise or forbid medical treatment or personal care decisions; it is limited to 'property and financial and business affairs'[49]. People who wish to make provision for personal care decisions should execute a living will[50].

The Court of Protection

If a patient has become incapable and no enduring power of attorney exists then that patient's affairs must be placed in the hands of the Court of Protection.

A medical certificate is necessary from a doctor stating that a patient is incapable by reason of mental disorder of managing and administering her property and affairs[51].

Normally the patient should be served with a notice of application though the court can dispense with this requirement if it is satisfied that the patient is incapable. The court will appoint a receiver (usually the nearest relative, or any relative who applies, or a friend, social worker, solicitor, etc).

If the value of the patient's property is less than £5,000 the 'short procedure' does not require the appointment of a receiver.

The court has exclusive control over all property and affairs of the patient. Guidance must be sought whenever anything not provided for in an existing order or directions needs to be done[52]. Again, the Court has no jurisdiction over the management and care of the patient's person, medical treatment, etc.

---

47. Section 8.
48. Re R (Enduring Power of Attorney) [1990] 2 WLR 1219.
49. Re F (Mental Patient: Sterilisation) [1989] 2 WLR 1025.
50. See Chapter 8.
51. Court of Protection Rules 1984, r 32.
52. Re W (EEM) [1971] Ch 123.

A person who does not have mental incapacity cannot execute a will. The court can make a statutory will in cases where mental incapacity exists[53]. The court must assume, in exercising its power to make a will for a person that the person would have been 'a normal decent person acting in accordance with contemporary standards of morality'[54]. Thus the court made valid lifetime gifts and executed a will on behalf of a woman who was born with severe mental disability but whose parents had left her a substantial amount of property.

Abuse of elderly people

Fifteen years ago, abuse of the elderly was rarely talked about and was hardly a recognised social problem. That is not, of course, to say that the problem did not exist or that the phenomena is new. Child abuse and matrimonial violence were also little talked about 15 years ago. Today they receive considerable media attention. Abuse of the elderly has not, yet at least, received the same sort of publicity. Lack of research in this area means that the extent of the problem, which most informed commentators recognise as a serious one, is unknown.

A definition

Abuse can, of course, take many forms. It can include all of the following types of behaviour[55]:

- physical assault including pushing, punching, pinching, slapping, forced feeding and forced medication;

- threats of physical assault;

- neglect, including locking the person in his room, refusing to supply meals, etc;

- psychological abuse, including shouting, screaming and abandonment, either to residential care or hospital;

- financial exploitation of finance or property;

- sexual abuse.

---

53. Mental Health Act 1983, s 95

54. *Re C (a spinster and patient)* (1991) *Independent* 2 February.

55. Eastman, M (1984) Old Age Abuse London: Age Concern.

56. See, eg *Independent*, 22 July 1987, *Guardian* 12 and 19 November 1986.

The abuser may not always be a relative. Revelations of elderly abuse occurring in residential homes are not uncommon[56]. Where abuse does exist, is the law's response adequate?

Legal constraints

Any form of abuse may constitute both a crime and/or a tort (civil wrong). The Offences Against the Person Act 1861 creates several offences which are relevant to this situation. For criminal liability to be incurred the prosecution must generally prove that the assailant intended to cause the victim harm. The different types of assault under the Act, ranging from the least to the most serious, are as follows:

- Assault occasioning actual bodily harm (s 47). This would include bruising, causing grazes to the skin, etc. Forcibly giving medication which results in bruising, for example, would be unlawful under this section.

- Inflicting bodily injury (s 20). This includes 'wounding' which is a breach of the whole skin or inflicting serious bodily harm, eg causing limbs to be broken.

- Causing grievous bodily harm (s 18) with intention to do such injury. Section 18 is the more serious offence and can be punished by life imprisonment whereas the maximum sentence under both ss 20 and 47 is five years' imprisonment. Verbal abuse causing the requisite degree of psychological harm might also fall within this section but the consequences of the verbal abuse would have to be extremely serious.

Section 23 makes it an offence to maliciously administer poison so as to endanger life or inflict grievous bodily harm and s 24 makes it a more serious offence if the perpetrator intends to cause the harm. Thus the forcible administration of medication could be an offence under one or other of these sections.

Whether it is appropriate to invoke the criminal law in cases of elderly abuse is, of course, debatable. Where such harm is inflicted by other than family members, eg by staff in a residential or nursing home, there should be less hesitation about using the criminal law to inflict retribution and as a deterrence.

Where the abuse takes the form of misappropriating the elderly person's property then an offence under the Theft Act 1968 could be committed.

Civil liability can arise in the tort of trespass, which includes assault (where a person has reasonable cause to fear that direct harm is to be directed at him, battery (actual, direct and intentional application of force) and false imprisonment

---

56. See, eg *Independent*, 22 July 1987, *Guardian* 12 and 19 November 1986.

(unauthorised physical restraint, eg locking a person in his room). Neglect could give rise to an action in negligence. The remedies available for victims are an action in damages and, in certain circumstances, an injunction may be obtained to prevent further abuse. Little is made, however, of these provisions. If the abuse takes place in a hospital or residential or nursing home the relevant complaints procedure can be invoked. Protective action, by removing the elderly person from the home, might be instituted under the Mental Health Act 1983, where relevant or under the National Assistance Act 1948, s 47 (see above).

Whether the law is equipped to deal with the problem is debatable. The answer to the problem must surely lie in trying to understand why is happens and thus adopt strategies for eliminating it.

CASE STUDY ONE

Mrs Anderson, aged 79, has been living with her daughter, Betty, and son-in-law Charles for two years since her husband's death. On the sale of her own home, Mrs Anderson gave her daughter and son-in-law £20,000 to build her a 'granny flat'. Over the past two years Mrs Anderson has become increasingly forgetful and 6 months ago she was diagnosed as suffering from Alzheimer's disease. Although the family have suggested to her that she go in to residential care, Mrs Anderson has adamantly refused. Caring for her is putting a considerable strain on the family and, to help provide them with some relief, arrangements have been made in the last two months for her to attend a day centre on two days per week. The staff at the day centre have become increasingly concerned that Mrs Anderson has regular, fresh bruises, over her body. When asked how these occurred, Mrs Anderson says she 'cannot remember, I must have knocked myself'. A social worker visits Betty to discuss with her the bruises, but her answers are evasive – 'she is always falling over, that is how they must have happened'. The social worker is worried that the bruising is in fact caused by non-accidental injury.

- What, if anything, can the social services department do?

- If Mrs Anderson refuses to go into residential care, can she be forced to do so?

- If she was admitted to residential care, who would pay? Her savings are now £8,000 as the money she had from the sale of her house has been used in her daughter's property.

CASE STUDY TWO

Mr Sidhu is aged 72 and has a wife, living in Norway, from whom he has long been estranged. They are, however, still married and there has never been a judicial separation. He also has a son aged 47. In 1991 Mr Sidhu began cohabiting with Mrs Tetley but two years later Mr Sidhu suffered a severe stroke and since that time has been a patient in a private hospital. The fees are paid by Mrs Tetley who has Mr Sidhu's power of attorney. Mr Sidhu lacks mental capacity. Mr Sidhu's son, Victor makes arrangements for Mr Sidhu to have his father flown to Norway by private plane. Mrs Tetley objects as she wishes to continue to make arrangements for his care herself.

Can Victor be prevented from removing his father from the hospital in such circumstances?

CASE STUDY THREE

Mrs Bentham is a resident in a private old people's home, her fees being paid for by the social services department. She has a history of depression and has, latterly, become increasingly confused. The arrangements for her admission were made by a daughter, Carol who visits regularly. Carol is becoming increasingly concerned that her sister, Daphne who lives in South America, plans to take her mother on holiday to South America as she refuses to accept that her mother is dementing. Carol is concerned that, if this did happen, her mother, Mrs Bentham, would be put at risk.

Can Carol, the local authority or the manager of the home prevent Mrs Bentham's removal in such circumstances?

Introduction

Health and safety legislation has a long history dating back to the beginning of the 19th century[1]. The purpose of the legislation from the outset has been to deter employers from employing workers in conditions which are dangerous or unhealthy. Employers in breach of their statutory obligations have, potentially, always been subject to criminal liability. During the 19th century civil liability also developed both in the tort of negligence where a worker injured by an employer's own negligence was able to recover compensation[2] and, since 1897[3] even without the need to prove fault or breach of duty by the employer[4]. Health and safety issues are of topical interest for health service professionals for a variety of reasons. Over-long working hours of junior hospital doctors, work-related stress disorders and the incidence of back injury among nurses have all been widely discussed. This chapter sets out the general law on health and safety at work and then focuses on specific issues of relevance and interest to nurses.

An outline of the general law

The Health and Safety at Work, etc Act 1974

The Robens Committee on Safety and Health at Work[5] was set up in 1970 to undertake a comprehensive review of the existing law and practices relating to health and safety. Its recommendations lead to the passing of the Health and Safety at Work, etc Act 1974 which is an extremely important modern and reforming piece of legislation. Enforcement of the provisions in the Act is by way of criminal sanctions; no civil liability is created and thus the pre-existing civil law remains in place. Originally health authorities were not bound by the health and safety legislation as the Crown has traditionally enjoyed immunity. This immunity was removed, after much criticism, by the National Health

---

1. Health and Morals of Apprentices Act 1802.
2. See, eg *Brydon v Stewart* [1855] 2 Macq 30.
3. Workmens' Compensation Act 1897.
4. The current law is contained in the National Assistance (Industrial Injuries) Act 1946.
5. Cmnd 5034.

Service and Community Care Act 1990 and the position now is that both health authorities and NHS trusts are fully bound by the legislation. Thus the legal rules applicable in this area have become of considerable relevance to the nursing profession.

Duties of employers under the Act

There is a general duty placed on employers 'to ensure, so far as is reasonably practicable, the health, safety and welfare at work of all his employees'[6]. People on work training programmes are now also covered by the legislation[7]. While this section appears potentially imprecise, an employer's duties are in fact complex and wide-ranging. Thus there is not only a duty to provider a safe workplace, but there is also a duty to provide a safe system of work. The Act also applies to people who are not employees if they are affected by activities which are being carried out in places of work.

In determining what is or is not 'reasonably practicable' the courts do attempt to assess whether the expense which would be involved in minimising or eradicating the risk is disproportionate to the actual risk[8]. The burden lies upon the defendant employer to show that it was not reasonably practicable to avoid the risk of injury. Whether a small employer is allowed to plead poverty in determining reasonable practicability is uncertain as the courts seem not to have addressed this issue. It would, however, seem unjust for the law to give less protection in this area to employees of small firms than it does to those working for multi-nationals, or in the public sector.

Written safety policy

All employers with five or more employees have a duty to prepare a written statement of their general policy on health and safety at work of their employees, and must bring the statement to the attention of their employees. There is no guidance in the legislation as to the contents of such a statement; the object is to ensure that employers sit down (in consultation with their safety representatives where relevant (see below)) and think about possible problems and solutions. Statements must be reviewed regularly to reflect any changes in the workplace and the risks inherent there.

---

6. Section 2(1).
7. The Health and Safety (Training for Employment) Regulations 1988, SI 1988/1222.
8. *Associated Dairies v Hartley* [1979] IRLR 171.

Enforcement provisions

The 1974 Act established a Health and Safety Commission (the HSC) and a Health and Safety Executive (the HSE). The Heath and Safety Commission is charged with the responsibility of, *inter alia*, encouraging and organising research, drawing up proposals for new legislation, approving Codes of Practice and laying down policy guidelines for the inspectorate. It makes annual reports to Parliament which contain statistics of occupational ill-health. The work-related diseases which are most commonly reported in Great Britain are general musculoskeletal conditions, hearing loss, stress and depression and lower respiratory disease. Many cases of occupational disease may well, of course, go undiagnosed, untreated or unreported. The line between occupational disease and non-occupational disease may, in practice, be difficult to draw. While there is a statutory obligation placed on employers to report to the HSE or local authorities accidents and dangerous occurrences at work and of work related disease[9] there is probably a considerable amount of under-reporting of non-fatal accidents[10].

The HSE is responsible to the HSC for enforcement of the law. Inspectors are appointed under the Health and Safety at Work, etc Act who are given wide ranging powers to enter and inspect premises and seize articles, substances and documents which may be needed as evidence in any proceedings for enforcement of the relevant statutory provisions[11]. These powers are arguably greater than those of a police constable. Local authority environmental health officers have similar powers in relation to shops, offices and catering establishments (which include nursing and residential homes for the elderly, disabled, etc). Health professionals' records and confidential medical records may be seized.

Where an inspector discovers a contravention of the law or a state of affairs which he considers highly dangerous he may issue an improvement or a prohibition notice. An improvement notice must identify the statutory provision which the inspector considers to have been infringed, state reasons why he believes it has been infringed and the time period in which the situation must be remedied[12]. A prohibition notice is served when an inspector is of the opinion that activities are, or are likely to be carried on involve a risk of serious personal injury[13]. The notice will order the discontinuance of the activity either with immediate effect (which is usual) or from a specified date.

---

9. Reporting of Injuries, Diseases and Dangerous Occurrences Regulations 1985, SI 1985/2023.

10. Labour Force Survey, 1990 reported that only 30 per cent of non-fatal injuries were reported to the HSE.

11. Health and Safety at Work, etc Act 1974, s 20.

12. Section 21

13. Section 22

An employer may appeal against either notice to an industrial tribunal which has the power to cancel, affirm or modify the notice. A further appeal lies to the High Court and then the House of Lords. Contravention of an improvement notice is a criminal offence punishable by a fine; contravention of a prohibition notice is punishable by imprisonment.

Penalties

The HSC, which has overall responsibility for policy matters, has made it clear that prosecutions should be regarded as a last resort. Section 33 sets out the circumstances under which offences can be committed. As well as the contravention of improvement and prohibition notices (see above), it is an offence to fail to discharge a general duty or to contravene any health and safety regulation, to obstruct an inspector, make a false statement forge a document, etc. Most offences may be tried in either the magistrates or the Crown Court. Magistrates can impose a maximum fine of £20,000 (£5,000 for lesser offences) whereas a Crown Court has unlimited powers to fine[14]. There are also powers to imprison under the Act but courts are extremely loath to make such orders and in cases where a prison sentence has been ordered, they have always been suspended.

Employees' obligations

The Health and Safety at Work, etc Act, s 7 imposes on employees a duty to take reasonable care for the health and safety, not only of themselves but of other persons who may be affected by their acts or omissions at work. Employees' conduct will, however, be judged in relation to the training given, the resources available and the level of authority which they enjoys. Furthermore, employees are under statutory duty to co-operate with their employer so that the employer can fulfil the obligations which the law imposes on him.

European Union obligations

Article 118A of the Treaty of Rome provides:

> Member States shall pay particular attention to encouraging improvements, especially in the working environment, as regards the health and safety of workers, and shall set as their objective the harmonisation of conditions in this area, while maintaining the improvements made.

This provision allows the legislative machinery of the European Union to issue directives on health and safety which all Member States (including the

---

14. The highest recorded fine is £750,00 imposed on BP as a result of fatalities at the Grangemouth Oil Refinery in 1988.

UK) are bound to give effect to. These directives[15] have lead to radical reform of the law in this area. The Management of Health and Safety at Work Regulations[16] implements the 'framework' directive[17] and provides an administrative mechanism, backed by enforcement procedures, to promote safety at work by preventing accidents and disease. The European Union regards legislation as the most effective means of protecting the workforce. The UK government philosophy throughout the 1980s and 1990s has been to place greater emphasis on self-regulation and de-regulation. While there is limited research in this area, that which has been undertaken does suggest that self-regulation which is not supported by external enforcement measures is less effective[18]. European Union law on health and safety issues is, however, binding and is unaffected by the UK's opt-out at Maastricht, of the Social Chapter. UK legislation must be interpreted to give effect to the directives[19].

A survey in the summer of 1994 undertaken by the Eagle Star Insurance Company demonstrated that three-quarters of companies were failing to comply with the six sets of regulations introduced in 1992 to comply with European Union law. This apparently widespread failure to implement the regulations means, presumably, that preventable accidents and injuries are continuing to occur.

Worker involvement in health and safety issues

The Robens Committee advocated in its report[20] worker involvement in health and safety issues as it believed that such involvement would reduce accidents at work. While enlightened employers had historically always involved their employees in these matters, the question arose as to whether this should be a mandatory requirement placed on all employers. Parliament incorporated into the health and safety legislation[21] a statutory obligation on employers which requires them to consult with workers only where there exists in the workplace a recognised trade union. A recognised trade union (and there is no machinery which exists to compel an employer to recognise a trade union) may appoint safety representatives[22] from among the workforce who have a right to reason-

---

15. See the following Directives: 89/31; 89/654; 89/655; 89/656; 90/269; 90/270; 91/383.
16. SI 1992/2051.
17. Directive 89/391.
18. See, eg S Dawson (1988) Safety at Work; the Limits of Self-regulation (1988) CUP.
19. *SA Marleasing v La Commercial Internacional de Alimentacion* [1990] (Case C-106/89 ECJ).
20. Cmnd 5034.
21. Health and Safety at Work, etc Act 1974, s 2.
22. Safety Representatives and Safety Committee Regulations 1977, SI 1977/500.

able time off with pay for relevant training[23]. The number which can be appointed is determined by[24] the total number of employees, the type of activity in which the employer is engaged and the risks involved.

The functions of the safety representative, in addition to representing employees and consulting with the employer are as follows[25]:

(i)   to investigate potential hazards and dangerous occurrences in the workplace (whether or not they are drawn to his attention by the employees he represents) and to examine the causes of accidents in the workplace;

(ii) to investigate complaints by any employee he represents relating to that employee's health, safety or welfare at work;

(iii) to make representations to the employer on matters arising in (i) and (ii) above;

(iv) to make representations to the employer on general matters affecting the health, safety or welfare at work of the employees at the workplace;

(v)   to carry out inspections of the workplace after giving the employer reasonable notice in writing (Regulation 5);

(vi) to represent the employees he was appointed to represent in consultations at the workplace with inspectors of the HSE and of any other enforcing authority;

(vii) to receive information from inspectors in accordance with s 28(8) of the 1974 Act; and

(viii) to attend meetings of safety committees where he attends in his capacity as a safety representative in connection with any of the above functions.

An employer must establish a safety committee if requested in writing to do so by two or more safety representatives. The functions of the safety committee[26] include the study of accidents, diseases, statistics and trends, so that reports can be made to management with recommendations for improvement; consideration of reports from the inspectorates and liaison with them; consideration of reports from safety representatives; assisting in the development of works safety rules and safe systems of work, etc.

---

23. Regulation 4(2).
24. HSE Code of Practice.
25. Regulation 4(1).
26. HSE Guidance Note.

Legal protection of employees in exercising health and safety rights

An employee has the right not to be subjected to a detriment (eg demoted or moved to a less attractive working environment or denied promotion)[27] or dismissed[28] in the following circumstances:

- having been designated by the employer to carry out activities in connection with preventing or reducing risks to health and safety at work, he carried out (or proposed to carry out) those activities;

- being a safety representative or member of a safety committee he performed (or proposed to perform) any functions as such;

- if there is no safety representative or safety committee where he is, or, if there are, it is not reasonably practicable to raise such matters, he brought the employer's attention (by reasonable means) to circumstances connected with his work which he reasonably believed were harmful or potentially harmful to health and safety;

- in circumstances of danger which he reasonably believed to be serious or imminent and which he could not reasonably be expected to avert, he left, or proposed to leave, or, while the danger persisted, he refused to return to, his place of work or any dangerous part of his place of work;

- in circumstances of danger which he reasonably be believed to be serious and imminent, he took, or proposed to take, appropriate steps to protect himself or other persons from the danger. This is to be judged by reference to all the circumstances, including his knowledge, and the facilities and advice available to him at the time. However, he will not have been subjected to a detriment/his dismissal will not be regarded as unfair if he was so negligent in the steps he took that the employer treated him as a reasonable employer would have treated him in those circumstances. These provisions derive from a European directive.

Complaints are heard by an industrial tribunal and compensation is available for both employees who have been subjected to a detriment and those who have been unfairly dismissed[29]. In addition, re-instatement or re-engagement may be ordered in the event of the employee being dismissed[30]. Furthermore, an employee who has been dismissed can apply to an industrial tribunal within

---

27. Employment Protection (Consolidation) Act 1978, s 22A.
28. Employment Protection (Consolidation) Act 1978, s 57A.
29. Employment Protection (Consolidation) Act 1978, ss 22C and 72.
30. Employment Protection (Consolidation) Act 1978, s 69.

seven days of the dismissal for 'interim relief'[31]. which allows the tribunal to order re-instatement, re-engagement or an order for continuation of the employment pending a final determination of the case. 'Interim relief' is an important remedy today when in ordinary cases an applicant to an industrial tribunal hearing can expect to wait many months for a full hearing.

Specific health and safety issues of concern to the nursing profession

With the development of European Union law in this area, there are a number of regulations which are specifically relevant to the nursing profession.

The Control of Substances Hazardous to Health (COSHH) Regulations

All potentially hazardous substances, whether or not they are specifically named in the regulations, are covered. In hospitals this will include, for example, chemicals, ionising radiation, etc. Under the regulations the employer has a duty to assess the risk and introduce controls which reduce exposure to those risks to the lowest level which is reasonably practicable. Where necessary employers must provide personal protective equipment but this must not be used as an alternative to reasonable controls to reduce the risk. Control mechanisms must be put in place to check that the controls are effective. Employees who are exposed to risks which may be harmful to their health are entitled to regular health checks. The Ionising Regulations 1985 require employers to medically examine employees who may be so exposed before or soon after their employment commences so that this can be used as a base-line for subsequent tests.

The obligations owed by the employer under these regulations are strict, ie there is no defence that all reasonable precautions were taken. An employee who is injured as a result of the employer's breach of the regulations can bring a civil action for compensation for breach of statutory duty.

The Manual Handling Regulations 1992

These regulations came into force on 1 January 1993 and provide that an employer shall, so far as is reasonably practicable, avoid the need for any of his employees to undertake any manual handling operations at work which involve a risk of their being injured. Manual handling means any transporting

---

31. Employment Protection (Consolidation) Act 1978, s 77.

or supporting of a load (including lifting, putting down, pushing, pulling, carrying or moving thereof) by hand or by bodily force. Where it is not reasonably practicable for an employee to avoid a manual handling operation the employer is under a duty to make an assessment of the risk having regard to the task, the loads, the working environment and individual capacity[32]. After assessing the risk the employer must take appropriate steps to reduce the risk of injury to the lowest possible level which is reasonably practicable.

These regulations are particularly relevant to nurses as quite clearly there are many occasions where the lifting of patients cannot be avoided. Nearly one-third of all accidents reported to the HSE in any one year arise from manual handling. It is estimated that one in four nurses suffer back pain at the end of each working day; some 3,600 nurses leave the profession each year because of back injury and 80,000 nurses take sick leave in any one year because of back injury. What impact the Regulations have on these statistics remains to be seen.

An employee has a duty under the regulations[33] to make full and proper use of any system of work provided for his use by his employer. Thus an employee who is injured at work as a result of his or her own failure to comply with the health and safety policies laid down by his employer may be precluded from claiming compensation for his or her injury.

Occupational stress and an employer's duty of care

Employers are under an obligation at common law to take such care for the health and safety of their employees so as not to expose them to a risk of injury. This common law obligation, breach of which will give rise to civil liability and thus a claim for compensation, imposes on employers a duty to provide a safe system of work, safe plant and equipment, and a safe place of work[34]. In 1994 UNISON, the public employees union, brought an action for compensation on behalf of one of their members, a social worker, who claimed that he had suffered a nervous breakdown as a result of pressure of work[35]. This was the first claim of its kind to be successful in the English courts. Mr Walker's claim was based on the argument that his employers had breached the common law duty of care they owed to him by failing to take steps to avoid exposing him to a health-endangering workload.

Why was Mr Walker's claim successful? First, the medical evidence available to the court indicated that he was a man of 'reasonable fortitude', that is, he was

---

32. Regulation 4.
33. Regulation 5.
34. *Wilsons & Clyde Coal Co Ltd v English* [1938] AC 57.
35. *Walker v Northumberland County Council* [1995] 1 All ER 737.

not a 'vulnerable personality'. Second, his family and social situation was not particularly stressful. Third, and probably most importantly, he had been working some 15 years as a social worker before his first breakdown and had tried to change his circumstances by making recommendations for change to his senior management which were not acted upon and thus the second breakdown which he suffered was foreseeable.

A junior hospital doctor has also recently made legal history by suing his employers for failure to protect his health and safety at work by requiring him to work over-long hours[36]. While the case ended in an out-of-court settlement (Dr Johnstone accepted £5,000) the Court of Appeal had accepted that there was at least an arguable case that the employers were liable. This decision could have considerable implications for employers, particularly health authorities and NHS trusts.

Conclusion

As can be seen, the development of health and safety law has been rapid over the last few years. Employers ignore it at their peril. Employees can expect to work in environments which are not a potential danger to their health and if they are forced to do so, can expect adequate compensation.

---

36. *Johnstone v Bloomsbury Health Authority* [1991] 2 All ER 293. See also 'To work, perchance to sleep' *Sunday Telegraph* 16 April.

CASE STUDY ONE

Mary is a trainee nurse at a district general hospital who has been told that she is not to lift a patient on her own. One day, whilst working on the ward she saw a large old lady lying on the floor in considerable pain. The only other nurse on the ward at that time was dealing with an emergency admission. Mary therefore lifted the patient onto the bed and as she did so felt a shooting pain in the region of her third lumbar vertebra. Since then she has been unable to work .

Consider the liability of the hospital.

CASE STUDY TWO

Jim is a nurse who has been employed on a geriatric ward in a district general hospital for the last three months. He has become extremely concerned about the staffing levels on the ward and feels that both staff and patients' safety is being compromised. He complains to the nursing officer who ignores his concerns. He then writes a letter to the local paper highlighting his concerns. He is summarily dismissed.

Advise Jim.

Index